PENGUIN BOOKS

KNITTING

Bartlett spent her childhood in rural South Australia. Whilst raising her four children, she worked as an editor, ghostwriter and feature writer, as well as knitting designer garments for boutiques. *Knitting* was written as the major component of a creative writing PhD, at the University of Adelaide. She lives with her husband, who has been a pastor for more than twenty years, in the Adelaide Hills.

knitting

anne bartlett

PENGUIN BOOKS

PENGUIN BOOKS

Published by the Penguin Group
Penguin Books Ltd, 80 Strand, London wc2r orl, England
Penguin Group (USA) Inc., 375 Hudson Street, New York, New York 10014, USA
Penguin Group (Canada), 90 Eglinton Avenue East, Suite 700, Toronto, Ontario, Canada m4p 2y3
(a division of Pearson Penguin Canada Inc.)
Penguin Ireland, 25 St Stephen's Green, Dublin 2, Ireland
(a division of Penguin Books Ltd)
Penguin Group (Australia), 250 Camberwell Road, Camberwell, Victoria 3124, Australia
(a division of Pearson Australia Group Pty Ltd)
Penguin Books India Pvt Ltd, 11 Community Centre, Panchsheel Park, New Delhi – 110 017, India
Penguin Group (NZ), 67 Apollo Drive, Rosedale, North Shore 0632, New Zealand
(a division of Pearson New Zealand Ltd)
Penguin Books (South Africa) (Pty) Ltd, 24 Sturdee Avenue,
Rosebank, Johannesburg 2196, South Africa

Penguin Books Ltd, Registered Offices: 80 Strand, London wc2r orl, England

www.penguin.com

First published by Houghton Mifflin Company, Boston & New York 2005
Published by Penguin Group (Australia) 2005
Published in Penguin Books 2007

1

Copyright © Anne Bartlett, 2005
All rights reserved

The moral right of the author has been asserted

Printed in England by Clays Ltd, St Ives plc

isbn: 978-0-141-02065-5

For my mother,
who gave me stories and knitting

CONTENTS

August

EVER SINCE Jack's funeral Sandra had been covered in glass. Not glass from an accident, shattered bits of windscreen or the hard razor-cut edges of a plate glass window. Nothing like that. Sandra was covered in a thick layer of elastic glass that stretched over her body like another skin, holding her in and keeping everybody else out. It moved with her wherever she went, invisible under her clothes, into the shower, into bed, into the sun, and kept her cold as ice. Friends knocked on it. She could hear them, but the glass was over her eyes, too, so that everything she saw was far away, even though she knew she could reach out and touch. She was covered in ice-cold glass and would never be warm again.

So when Sandra saw the gaudy envelope in the letter box, her heart sank. She knew what it was—her invitation to the annual dinner she and a group of school friends had maintained for over thirty years. She would have to go, of course; she couldn't not go, but she dreaded it all the same.

Another item on the list called First Meetings Post Jack. More hugging and caring and how-are-you-getting-on to negotiate. The first widow among them, an object of compassion, confrontation, and curiosity. *How do you think she's dealing with it? Not too badly. Immersed herself in work.* And what she couldn't tell them, hadn't told anyone, was that her days were as dry-eyed as a desert. She didn't know how to weep.

She reluctantly tore open the envelope and propped the invitation on the mantelpiece. Over the years they had tried a vast range of restaurants. This one would require a new dress.

THAT same afternoon Martha McKenzie walked down Muggs Hill Road, her strawberry hair glowing in the meek offering of the South Australian winter sun. She was rugged in her overcoat, and as usual she carried her three big bags: the expandable striped bag, the tapestry carpet-bag, and the old brown suitcase. As she approached the corner near the bus stop something shimmering caught her attention. The shimmering was in front of a small bluestone church that Martha had passed hundreds of times but never entered.

Martha was not in the habit of going to church. She was forty-seven years old and hadn't needed church yet, nor it her. Martha was decidedly uninterested in churches; the last time she had been to church she was ten years old and had bitten an old man on the hand, for good reason.

She was long-sighted, but she wore her glasses now for knitting. She squinted at the shimmering. Martha liked things to be right side up and comprehensible, though some things, she knew, could not be explained. This was like a heat haze or the flummery flow of air above a gas pump on a hot day.

Martha looked carefully left and right down the narrow street, then tramped across it to the church. Here she was distracted by something else. Above the steps leading up to the front porch was a heavy wooden door, cheerfully painted but firmly shut, and on the door was a HELP WANTED sign, with a phone number and a cartoon of a woman with a vacuum cleaner.

Martha sat heavily on the church steps — her knees gave her trouble in winter — to think about it, but she kept her fingers resting on the handles of her bags in case something untoward happened.

The high column of shimmering was to her left, half over a cement path and half over a rose bed abutting the path. The silvery light didn't seem to mind the prickly bare sticks of wintering roses; it moved and flowed among them without proper regard for itself.

Like a waterfall, thought Martha, only nothing gets wet. She sat there watching it, her mind busy with other thoughts. Sometimes so many thoughts buzzed in her brain she felt as if she had a beehive on her shoulders instead of a head. This morning the buzzing was mild and had to do with the rose bushes in front of her, cleaning a church, and rectifying her current knitting problem, a complex lace pattern she had not been able to get right. Martha loved roses and noted that these needed pruning, but she couldn't concentrate on anything properly. It was hard to concentrate when everything around seemed to sparkle. Then, in a moment of clarity, like a knot that untangles itself when tugged at both ends, the knitting problem resolved.

Martha stood up, reread the notice on the church door, then tore it off and put it in the side pocket of one of her commodious bags. She closed her fingers around the handles—she had barely let go of two of them—stood stiffly and went home.

SANDRA was reading in the study she had once shared with Jack. Outside it was cold and getting dark. It was already dark and cold inside, except for this room, the smallest room at the back of the house. The study was easy to keep warm; there was no point in warming the whole house for one person.

To her left was a pile of books on ancient textiles and a stack of tagged journal articles waiting to be read. To her right was a neat tray of work completed: essays marked, forms filled out, a letter supporting a student's application for scholarship extension.

Even here Sandra was spare with the heating. She wore thick socks, a heavy jumper, and a jacket over that, but her fingers were still cold. *Wear wool,* said Sandra's mother across fifty years of living, *Wear that woollen jumper I made you—it's much warmer.* But in spite of her fascination with textiles, Sandra had dismissed the comfort and warmth of wool long ago. Wool was too slow, too impractical for a modern world: it might be machine washable but it still ruined in the dryer. Wool was too romantic, too pastoral—too innocent. The nursery rhymes about sheep—Baa Baa Black Sheep, Little Bo Peep—all had happy endings. Wool was just one of the many textiles she had studied over the years. It was durable if you could keep the moths out, but she had no personal interest in it. Wool was noteworthy as a phenomenon, but not viable in Sandra's fast and busy world. As for Australia riding on the sheep's back, those days were over.

It was ten months since Jack's death. After the chaos caused by his illness and the many changes in learning to be single again, Sandra was pretending that she led an ordered life. Her desk was clear except for the papers in use, her books straight and easy in their orderly rows, the bulletin board uncluttered. She had covered the flat, bleak surface of Jack's empty desk with potted plants and piles of books, but the plants failed to thrive and the books were those she never read.

Her screen saver resolved into Jack's face. He smiled at her from under his cotton sun hat and above his favorite woollen jacket, made by a local weaver. His face was crinkled against the wind blowing that day on the top of Mount Buffalo; the stubbly beard showed new grey. It wasn't a particularly well-composed photo, but it caught the light in his dark eyes, the lurking amusement that had stopped Sandra from taking herself too seriously. On difficult days she turned the screen saver off so she could get on with her work. Jack's photo was one of many available on the program's random choice, but sometimes the timing was terrible.

On the wall opposite the computer was a print of Frederic Cotman's *One of the Family*, oil on canvas, 1880. Jack, the impossible romantic, had loved that painting, the suffused golden light, the cosy family sitting down to lunch, the interplay of action and relationship, the ridiculous horse at the door. But to Sandra it had seemed a mockery, a kind of pretence, something longed for but unattainable. It looked warm and soft and comfortable, like an old cotton dress, but reality was different. Reality was a cotton dress too small, buttons lost and seams fraying into holes.

After Jack died, Sandra took the painting down from the dining room wall, but when she tried to carry it out to the shed, somehow it wouldn't go. So, although she hadn't liked it for more than twenty years — ever since it became clear that they would have no children — she took it to her study and hung it on the wall at her back. There, she had said to Jack's reappearing photo, with the grim amusement that got her through the days: I don't like it, but have it if you want.

Jack, like Sandra, had begun academic life as a historian. Since those early years their paths had diverged: Sandra had begun with war history and moved easily to feminism and perceptions of women's work, then concentrated on textiles. Jack had made an even bigger shift: his interest in the impact of white settlement on local Aboriginal populations had evolved into a committed amateur interest in the threatened bird species of southern Australia. Jack might have been romantic, but when it came to disappearing birds he was an utter pragmatist. Driven by alarm at the rapid rate of species extinction, he had been a keen volunteer on revegetation programs, both locally in the Adelaide Hills and farther north, where the introduced rabbits, sheep, and goats had decimated the natural habitat. Eventually his hobby dominated his work; his research was inventive, his record-keeping thorough, his books and journal articles internationally respected. In a climate of environmental pessimism he worked hard and hopefully for the future, developing action plans for the preservation and reintroduction of birds like the diamond firetail and the Mount Lofty Ranges spotted quail-thrush.

Jack worked for the future but lived thoroughly in the present. Sandra had seen how every chance finding of even common feathers gave him a little rush of pleasure. She did not share his fascination—another magpie feather, another wattlebird killed by a cat—but she envied his delight. With more unusual feathers his wide mouth wreathed into smiles, his brown fingers pressed and smoothed. Such simple access to joy. Her own life seemed complicated, her pleasures always one step removed.

After Jack died, Sandra opened the big box of feathers he had collected on their walks. For a week or two she left them lying about on the coffee table, though some broke free and drifted around the room, reminding her of past conversations with Jack—*elegance, strength, protection.* Could they be displayed somehow? She scooped them back into the box and took them to Martin, a picture framer who had been a close friend of Jack's. When she returned to pick up the one framing she had ordered, he presented her with a large package. A gift, he said, in memory of Jack. Open it at home. And waved away her purse.

When Sandra lined up the framed pieces along the skirting board in her living room, she saw that Martin had reworked her meagre idea into something far greater. The six pieces, individually simple, became something more in juxtaposition, a mass of wings beating upward, gathering into flight.

The following weekend Martin came to hang them for her. Sandra took him to the bedroom, hoping he would not think her sentimental. Here, she said, around the bed. Martin set to work. As she passed him the first piece, she suddenly noticed the neat inscription in fine silver writing on the back: Jack Fildes/Martin Shepherd: *Series 1/6, Wings*.

But here she was, distracted again. Sandra frowned and turned back to the computer. The screen saver flicked on, another rogue photo from one of Jack's albums. A cemetery, of all things, and through the middle, focused and clear, a carpet of thousands of red roses. Jack and his digital camera. Almost a year now, and new photos still appearing from nowhere.

She turned back to the journal article she had been reading: "Textile Artifacts of Ancient Greece". Perhaps this would stop her from thinking about Jack.

MARTHA had been out all day and was glad to be nearly home. The wind flapped at her buttoned coat and tugged at her bags. She liked this last stretch of the walk at this time of evening, watching parents coming home from work, children carrying sports clothes, dining room tables lit before the blinds came down. In summer, elderly Greek and Italian couples sat on their front verandas and nodded hello, but now, in winter, they were tucked into warm kitchens at the back. Martha imagined them serving dinner, moussaka and pasta.

Martha was carrying the usual three bags plus a shopping bag bulging with butternut and potatoes and a nice meaty bone she had found at the market. It had been a long day, and she looked forward to wrapping herself around some soup. After the soup she would have that bit of leftover apple pie made with apples from the family farm, and then, when she had done her dishes and made a nice pot of tea, she would sit at the kitchen table and read the knitting magazine she had just bought at the newsagent. It had a new technique that she had never tried, a fancy kind of slipstitch, and her fingers were itching for it.

SANDRA leaned back from her desk and sighed. For all her facility with words, she was not able to articulate what she found so fascinating in these ancient objects. These fragments of women's work had survived for thousands of years: tiny bits of cloth and hand tools—spindles, whorls, loom weights. Things made from the earth: clay, bone, stone, soapstone, gold, even, trapped in dirt and dust no broom had swept away. She could never imagine her own work surviving so long.

But these women from the ancient past, working in their own clear present, would not have expected permanence either. What spinner or weaver would have believed such fragile things could last as long as this? Even now the warp and weft of the cloth were clearly visible, fourteen threads to the centimeter, evenly spaced. Sturdy, everyday linen, wrapped around a dagger to protect it from damp, put aside for a week or a month, dug up after millennia.

Beautiful tools. Slender lengths and rounded weights, the beauty and necessity of balance, allowing the long thread from the distaff to be spun evenly by thumb and forefinger. Some of the smaller spindles for cotton and linen weighed only a few grams. And incised on the top of some was the concentric circle, the god's eye, for protection.

Sandra was not good with her hands. Her mother's small, stubby fingers had been surprisingly deft: they held the finest thread with delicacy, were precise with a needle. She had wanted to share these skills with Sandra, but Sandra was clumsy with needlework, no better with knitting. Besides, she wanted to be different from her mother.

However, in recent years her research had generated deep longing. Women who shared domestic necessities — food gathering, cloth making, medicine preparation, life-giving work compatible with child care — seemed to lead more integrated lives than she herself experienced. Alone now, husbandless, motherless, childless, she wanted to re-connect with some kind of community, with the long line of women and their work. Impossibly romantic, of course — she must have caught it from Jack. She was living in the twenty-first century, she had a laptop, she was connected to the whole world via the Internet. More "community" than the ancients could ever have imagined.

But it would be fun to follow her heart for once, to do something different from the usual round of lectures and articles. Mount an exhibition, perhaps — women's work, clothing of some kind. Nothing grand, a love job to fill a simple space somewhere, a small celebration of domestic work, the meanings of domestic cloth. Nothing too demanding or serious. She could play curator.

Besides, it would occupy her, give her a new project to fill some of the gaping hole left by Jack. And she could include her own craft, writing, somehow. Clothing interspersed with text. She felt fragments of idea cluster towards possibility. That textiles conference coming up in Wollongong—perhaps she would go after all. Maybe things would become clearer then.

MARTHA put the soup to boil, then unfolded the paper she had taken from the church door. She would rather clean a house than a church, but a church had happened along, so she might as well apply and see what came of it. And the location suited her, it was on her bus route into town, just before the South Parklands, which bordered the square-mile grid of the city proper. In fact she could walk into the city from the church if she wanted.

The fact was, she needed a job; if you wanted to keep knitting with something as exotic as cashmere you had to find the funds. Well, it might be silk. Or lambswool. She still hadn't decided, but whichever she chose, it would be expensive. She dialled the number on the paper.

A pleasant voice answered. "Kate Linkett."

"My name is Martha McKenzie. I've rung about the job."

"Job?"

"The cleaning job. At the church."

"Oh, yes. Sorry, I'm not really with it today. Are you free for an interview next Thursday?"

Martha was. Half an hour later the pleasant voice phoned back and confirmed the appointment. Five-thirty next Thursday at the back of the church, through the door marked OFFICE.

SANDRA had had a good dream, though it was receding quickly now. Ambushed again in her sleep. Jack wasn't here. Jack would never be here again.

She and Jack always slept in on Saturdays, had a slow breakfast together over the paper, coffee and something different from the daily muesli and toast — croissants, bagels, bacon with tomatoes from the garden. By the time breakfast was over, the washing was finished. They would hang it out together, then do the housework in one hour flat, Jack the upstairs and the bathrooms, Sandra the kitchen, dining room, living room, and both verandas.

Jack's illness had been totally unexpected. A walker, climber, swimmer, always the fitter of the two, Jack had collapsed when they were on holidays, dawdling pleasantly at Sydney's Circular Quay. After it became clear that he was seriously ill, Sandra hired cleaning help for a while, but she found it more intrusive than useful, feeling she must tidy for the cleaner, embarrassed by tissues in the bin and toothpaste on the vanity. Jack, more relaxed, said, "That's her job. We pay her to clean up our mess!" Sandra could never shake the sense that she was being spied on, that her personal details were laughed over in some cleaning women's union. As Jack grew thinner and more and more fatigued, Sandra resented any intrusion on what she knew must be their last days together. Three weeks before Jack died, she terminated the cleaner's services and moved their bedroom downstairs to the dining room, with the French doors open to the deck and the sun.

The house needed cleaning now, but what was the point? Who would ever see? She should do some shopping too, but there were a few stalwarts in the cupboard: baked beans, packaged soups, a can of corn.

She turned over and felt for Jack's pyjamas under his pillow. She still hadn't washed them, though after all these months they couldn't really smell of him. It was simply the fabric, the worn flannel, the sense of his touch. Her sharp practical side told her to get out of bed and throw everything in the washing machine, Jack's pyjamas included. That self was loud and necessary: it got her through work, it prepared lectures, it kept people at bay. But the real strength, Sandra knew, was with her other self, the soft sad one, the one that was allowed out only on weekends, the self that would keep her in bed until well after lunch.

She turned her face into the pillow. On the walls around her bed the feathers strained upward towards light.

SEVERAL suburbs away from Sandra's two-storey stone house, Martha lived frugally in a small flat just beyond the parklands. Malcolm, her brother, had helped her buy it, a few years before the young and beautiful discovered how good it was to live so close to the city, within walking distance of work, shops, restaurants and clubs. Martha was an orderly woman, though something about her, the way she shrugged her shoulders into her cardigan or tied her laces in floppy bows, may have suggested looseness, a lack of personal discipline. People would have been surprised, given first impressions, to enter Martha's kitchen and see the angle of her cutting board, just so on the counter, the shininess of her neat cutlery stacks in the second drawer, the ball of string secured with a red rubber band, the box of old waistband elastics pinned neatly into themselves.

In the evenings Martha listened to Radio National, to the news and concert music she liked, though she couldn't have said why. Even difficult music had a pattern to it if you listened hard enough. Until three weeks ago she had had a portable TV, but she had spontaneously given it to an Iraqi refugee family who had moved in two doors up, so the kids could watch *Play School* and the parents could learn English. She missed the hospital soaps, but never mind; she'd get another TV sometime. If there was a program she particularly wanted to see, she could always take her knitting in to Mary Sherbet next door. Mary Sherbet was always glad of company.

Meanwhile she had plenty to do. She had begun

working on a hot pink nylon toilet-roll cover and had almost finished a tea cosy. The nylon was unpleasant to work; although Martha took a certain delight in the shocking effect of the hot pink, her hands recoiled from the harsh touch of the synthetic yarn. The tea cosy was better, a sturdy wool with a tight twist, but a little wiry nonetheless. It wasn't quite finished; she hadn't sewn it up or darned in the loose ends. Sewing up was a boring job; she would do that another day when she had company to help the time pass more quickly.

Three weeks ago she had begun a silver-grey shawl, cashmere and wool, soft and lacy as cobweb. Working on this made her hands happy, and her heart too. She wondered who the recipient would be—she rarely knew when she started a garment. Experience had taught her that the owner would soon appear one way or another.

Knitting was the one thing Martha could do better than anyone else. Until quite recently she had knitted for a nationally known designer, making one-of-a-kind patterns for the rich and famous, but the pay had been meagre, the patterns complex, and she had been under continual pressure to complete garments quickly for a demanding market. Martha had enjoyed the work at first, the affirmation of being one of the few chosen from among the hundreds of knitters who had sent in sample swatches, but after a few years the careful pleasure she cherished in her knitting had leaked away. She began having violent nightmares about knitting needles and crochet hooks, and woke tired and dispirited. Her body ached. It was hard to do anything; her knitting had become mechanical, she felt like a robot. Eventually, with a desperate effort motivated by a terrible fear of another spell in hospital, she gathered all her courage into one phone call and announced her resignation. The designer, angered at losing her best knitter, argued, cajoled, and eventually offered more money, but Martha wouldn't budge.

"No, I'm knitting a shawl. And I want to make a tea cosy." The designer did not hear the desperation.

"A tea cosy! With your talent!"

"Oh, it takes some talent. I'm making up the pattern myself. It's in the shape of a cottage, with a blue front door, and two little knitted people leaning out the window. And I'm also knitting a pink nylon toilet-roll cover." Martha's agitation made her feel like vomiting. The words tumbled out of her mouth like stitches pulled from the needle.

The designer had choked with rage.

"Oh, Martha, what a waste! Martha, Martha! All the famous people lining up for your garments because they are so well made and so well finished! Nobody finishes as well as you."

"I know. That's what I'm doing now. Finishing. Goodbye." Too afraid to talk longer, Martha had hung up and stood breathing hard by the phone, resisting the urge to lift the handset, to apologise, to offer back her services.

She hated to disappoint people. Disappointing people was hard and terrible work, and she hoped she never had to do it again. For the next two hours she had lain on the bed, practising slow breathing, until she felt calm enough to go to her workroom and get out her pattern books.

Martha rarely knitted a pattern as it was written, though once she had decided on what was needed she liked to get it perfect. She hadn't yet finished the shawl, but she liked to read while she knitted, and now that the shawl was almost done it was time to think ahead for the next item, though she had no ideas yet.

After dinner Martha brewed her pot of tea and took out the new knitting magazine to read while she finished the last few rows; the shawl pattern was knitted into her brain now. The tea cosy was to put away against Christmas, a gift for her brother's wife, who had a teapot collection. The toilet-roll holder was a special request from Mary Sherbet. Mary Sherbet could knit—Martha had helped her learn so that she would have something to do with her hands when she gave up smoking—but this pattern was still beyond her. Martha didn't like either the cosy or the roll holder, but at least they were gifts of love.

For once Sandra started her Saturday early. She needed to buy a new dress for the reunion dinner. She hadn't bought anything since before Jack died, and it was about time she made an effort. In fact she hadn't worn a dress since Jack died. The dresses had stayed in their wardrobe,

lined up like ghostly versions of a different self. All winter
she had lived in three pairs of pants — jeans, black go-any-
wheres, and tracksuit pants. She hadn't worn any jewellery
either, except her engagement and wedding rings. She'd
kept her hair cut — her job demanded some attention to
appearance — but her makeup was minimal.

She didn't go out much these days. One night, samba
playing, midnight again, she had waxed her legs and
painted her nails bright red. She had drawn red bow lips
on her mouth to match her nails and coloured them in
with a lipstick called Seduction, then gone to bed in her
black negligee and lain on the white sheet flat on her back,
legs together and hands palm down on the mattress. She
had gone to sleep and dreamt she was crying, and when
she woke the pillow was wet. The next morning she saw
her smeared red lips in the mirror, looked down at her fin-
gernails in disgust, and spilt the polish remover in her
angry hurry to dissolve whatever it was that had got into
her the night before.

But that was weeks ago, and she had given herself a
talking-to. It was a nice day, it was time to buy a dress, and
never mind how you feel, the world hasn't come to an end
after all, so you might as well get on with it. Today at least.

By four o'clock that afternoon Sandra hadn't found a
dress. Even though it was still winter, every rack was unexpectedly bulging with spring stock, and she couldn't find
what she wanted. The shops would close in less than an
hour, and she was hurrying to try one more shop at the far

end of the street. She crossed Rundle Mall and re-entered the surging crowd, only to be stopped suddenly by the sight of a red-haired woman kneeling directly in her path, surrounded by three large bags. The late-afternoon crowd parted on either side, looked with curiosity, but barely slowed down. As Sandra tried to manoeuvre past, she saw that lying among the bags was a pair of feet in odd socks and dirty white sneakers. The woman was trying to rouse their owner, who was apparently unconscious. Sandra was going to pass them by—it was no concern of hers. She took three steps past them, but then turned back. The desperate look on the woman's face had demanded a response. She, Sandra, must have looked like that when Jack collapsed.

So instead of buying a dress, Sandra knelt on the paving bricks and felt at the man's throat for his pulse. His back was arched and he was shuddering, but his pulse was strong enough.

"Let's get him onto his side. Don't want him to choke." She instructed the woman to take hold of his leg, while she took hold of the old red spray jacket at the shoulder. Together they heaved him over. Now that someone had taken responsibility, a small crowd gathered to watch.

Sandra fished in her handbag for her mobile and phoned 000. While she was giving the details, the man stopped shaking and opened his eyes, though he looked dazed and unfocused. When she finished the call, she asked the woman if she knew him. She shook her head.

They waited a few minutes without talking. Sandra's

mind careered around in amazement, trying to absorb the fact that after so many months alone, her private life was suddenly directly involved in the hurly-burly of other people's lives. There was something disarming about this other person who had stopped to help a stranger, the woman with the red hair and the hand-knitted jumper with a picture of a farm scene on the front, who patted the man's back and spoke quietly in his ear to tell him the ambulance was coming. When it came, Sandra listened to the paramedics' questions, but they elicited no new information; the man had been walking along and just collapsed to the ground. The paramedics, unhurried but efficient enough, took notes and were finished in a few minutes. Sandra helped hoist the woman's three large bags into the ambulance. They were heavy.

As the door was closing, Sandra pulled her card out of her wallet, scribbled her home phone number on the back, and thrust it through the window.

"Let me know how he gets on," she said. The woman waved assent. Sandra looked around at the dispersing crowd. Plenty of people had time to stop if they didn't have to get involved.

SHE hadn't bought a dress but had run home for a quick shower and gone to the dinner anyway, black pants as usual. She was the last to arrive. Everyone seemed determined to have fun, and no one treated her any differently. Perhaps they had discussed it beforehand. As usual she enjoyed their differences, the cross-section of politics and preferences, the fact that no one in the group could get away with even the slightest pretension without causing raucous laughter.

She'd kept in touch with all of them but was closest to Kate. At school Sandra and Kate had been little more than acquaintances until they shared a project on feminism and became firm friends. They read Germaine Greer together in the bath and organised a secret bra-burning ceremony at two o'clock one morning, joined by the others. It was a decade late, but nobody minded that. Kate, a tall, plain girl who was well endowed and always surrounded by boys, soon discovered that bralessness was not practical, but Sandra found a new freedom that she rarely relinquished.

Kate now ran a quilting supply shop. She was married to Tony, a businessman, and had had one child, Jeremy, after several miscarriages. With some disappointment Sandra had watched her mellow over the years. Something had happened to Kate, though it was hard to say what exactly. She no longer needed to shout.

The first wedding dress Kate had made was for Sandra, a gift of love and service that the young and independent Sandra found hard to accept. Years ago she had spent a semester in one of Kate's quilting classes. Kate was a good teacher, but Sandra was no good at sewing. The fabric rucked, the seams were out of line, the thread broke, and her quilt remained unfinished.

"I'm hopeless," she had said to Kate, laughing and frustrated all at once.

"Ah, but look what you do with words," Kate had replied. "You're so patient and methodical. Remember that time you spent half a day getting a sentence right? You nearly drove me nuts."

Kate's life in her work-from-home studio seemed simpler to Sandra than her own, free as it was from academic politics and budget cuts and the demands, even occasional threats, of immature students. Kate was a gardener, an interest she and Sandra shared, but she was also community worker, former state president of Nursing Mothers, secretary of Parents and Friends, and active in a church agency to aid refugees. She rose early and went to bed early and achieved a great deal without rush or impatience.

Kate had a steel edge to her, though. Mellow though she now was, she had, once or twice over the years, gently confronted Sandra in a way that Sandra had found surprising and difficult.

The dinner was good, the food pleasingly presented. The wine loosened them and they laughed till the tears ran. It was good to be out with friends again.

When she got home she was too wired to sleep, so she put on her track pants and cleaned the house. When she finally did go to bed, the last image before sleep was of the woman she had met earlier that day — her round face, unruly hair piled loosely in a bun, her pleading look transforming into a smile of relief as she realised that at last someone in all the crowd was going to stop and help. Such an ordinary, plain-looking woman, suddenly beautiful.

THE next morning Martha sat knitting in the hospital ward with her bags at her feet, counting stitches in her head and studying the sleeping face of the man she had rescued. He wasn't as old as she had first thought. There was no grey in his stubble, and his face, relaxed in sleep, was relatively unlined. Early forties maybe. The five other beds in the ward were full of coughing, wheezing old men. They were all watching her and pretending they weren't. The name board over the bed said CLIFF FORD.

He opened his eyes.

"Who are you?"

"Martha McKenzie."

He looked away, trying to think, then looked back again.

"Do I know you?"

"Well, you do now. You fell over in the street. Another lady and me got you into an ambulance."

He looked away again.

"Thanks."

"Is that really your name?" said Martha. "Cliff Ford? Or is it half your name, as in Clifford? Have they left off your last name?"

"I know not how to tell thee who I am," quoted Cliff. "My name, dear saint, is hateful to myself. Romeo, I think." He closed his eyes again. "Doesn't matter," he went on vaguely. "Don't care really. What are you knitting?"

"A shawl," said Martha.

"Who's it for?"

"Don't know," said Martha.

"We're two of a kind," said Cliff, grinning suddenly. He was missing a lot of teeth. "Don't know or care much, do we?"

"I know plenty," said Martha. "And I care about you. I came to see how you are."

"Well, I'm all right, as you can see. But I could do with some underpants. I do not care for what I wear." He tugged at the hospital gown.

"I could get you some."

"No, no. Haven't got any cash."

"Don't worry about that. I've got money." There was a pause.

"Are you from the church?" asked Cliff suddenly.

"What church?"

"That one on Muggs Hill Road. I wrote it on the hospital form."

"No," said Martha. "But I know the one. I walk down that road all the time. Do you live near there?"

"There and everywhere," said Cliff.

"Do they know what's wrong with you yet?"

"No. Tests tomorrow."

"I'll come back," said Martha, rolling up her knitting. "And I'll bring you some underpants."

"Thank you."

Martha picked up her bags and made for the door. At the last minute she turned and smiled at him, then hurried away. She wanted to get home, have some dinner, and finish this piece. She knew now who it was for.

Several hours later, after knitting for nearly an hour, Martha felt her heart beginning to pound. Something was wrong with the shawl pattern, right now at the end, when she was on the third-to-last row. She had made a mistake. She should have been concentrating, not reading that magazine at the same time. She'd *taken her mind off the job* and now she'd *made a big mistake*. She could feel her forehead starting to sweat and that horrible prickly feeling at the base of her skull. *It doesn't matter,* she said to herself, *it's only a bit of knitting. Calm down and work it out.* But her heart was thumping away as though she'd had a big fright, and her head was getting more and more confused as she thought about all the hours she'd put into this shawl, and how beautiful it was, and how it was now ruined. And then she saw it. She'd done three purls instead of four back at the beginning of the row, and it was all right, she could fix it after all, undo one row stitch by stitch, and reknit it. It was beautiful yarn, this, and even though it was fine it was well twisted, so it unpicked easily.

Martha's heart didn't stop thumping until she had un-picked and reknitted the row. And then she proceeded with great care and concentration, not allowing herself to get distracted by reading patterns. She was too close to the end to take such silly risks.

But as she knitted, slowly and carefully now, she did spare a thought for that woman who had helped, the short woman with the trendy haircut and the diamond ring like a hard, sharp rock. It had caught on Martha's hand as they turned the man over, and scratched her. She must be very rich. But she had a sad blank face that didn't give much away.

SANDRA shocked herself by sleeping in on Sunday until nearly midday. It was a long time since she had relaxed enough to sleep more than five hours at once. At one o'clock the phone rang. When she answered it there was silence, followed by the clatter of coins in a public tele-phone. Did people still use coins? She didn't recognise the voice.

"Hello? Hello? Is that Sandra Fildes?"

"Speaking." How raspy her voice was. The other per-son hesitated.

"My name is Martha. You helped me yesterday when that poor bloke fell over in the mall. I just wanted to say thank you." Sandra was still groggy with sleep and strug-gled to respond.

"You're welcome."

"He's getting better. I went this morning. They're keeping him in for tests and stuff, but he's likely to walk out. Strikes me as one of those who hates being cooped up."

"Do they know what happened?"

"No. Epilepsy, maybe. Had a cousin with epilepsy, and it was a bit like that."

"Are you going back to see him?"

"Yes."

"Well, give him my best wishes." There was a rumble of traffic at Martha's end. Sandra had to repeat her best wishes.

"Don't think he'll remember you," shouted Martha. "He was out of it."

"Well, tell him anyway. Thank you for ringing."

"Wait!" Silence. What was the woman doing—fossicking in one of her bags? How to politely close this call?

"Would you mind if I came round?"

"Came round? Here?"

"Yes. To see you."

"Oh, it's not necessary. You've thanked me already."

"I've got something for you."

"I didn't really do anything. I was just there at the time. Truly, there's no need."

"There were lots of other people, but you were the only one who helped. It's OK, no trouble. I won't stay long. See you soon." Martha hung up.

Sandra was not happy. She was private about her personal space. She didn't really want anyone, especially a stranger, possible weirdo, giving her unwanted gifts. She had given the woman her card, with her home address on it. Why on earth had she done that?

She plumped the cushions by the phone, washed her lunch dishes, and waited, increasingly irritable, for Martha to show. She wanted to get it over with. *Soon*, Martha had said. So why didn't she come? Where was she coming from? And how? The buses ran infrequently—she looked like a bus person. Perhaps she'd changed her mind. Maybe Sandra had sounded unfriendly and put her off. The woman only wanted to express some thanks. She should have made more of an effort—Jack always said she was prickly with strangers. Sandra went back to the biography sent to her for review, but it had soured; the end wasn't as good as the beginning.

BY SEVEN o'clock Sandra decided that Martha wasn't coming after all and made herself a toasted cheese sandwich for tea. It was getting dark and cold. She sat in the half light of the window to eat. As she took the first bite the bell rang.

Sandra opened the door reluctantly. The woman stood there hesitantly, not looking her entirely in the face.

"I'm Martha. I'm a bit late." No apology.

"Come in." Sandra was hardly effusive. The woman turned sideways to carry a small suitcase and two large bags over the threshold, then stood there waiting. She was wearing a denim skirt and another hand knit, an old-fashioned pale pink jumper in a complex pattern. Her shoes were flat walkers. She sighed a hefty sigh and said, "Smells nice."

"It's not much. Just a toasted sandwich."

Martha stood, holding her bags. Sandra could hear Jack's voice in her head. *Come on, Sandra, be kind.*

"Come in." Sandra turned on the light in the cold living room. She sat on the edge of her chair and invited Martha to sit down. Martha positioned her three bags carefully in a row and sank heavily into the leather. Sandra waited.

"I was at the hospital. Cliff says thanks."

"You say you never met him?"

"Nup. Never. Poor old bugger was just lying there rattling his teeth and nobody did anything. Except you and me."

Sandra felt ashamed.

"Would you like a snack?"

"Wouldn't say no."

"Come out and talk to me while I make it." She didn't want to leave this woman where she couldn't see her. Who knows what she might stuff in her bags? Martha followed her obediently, bringing her luggage. Sandra re-oiled the sandwich grill.

"Pretty fancy kitchen you've got."

"Yes. Don't really use it enough these days."

"You live here by yourself?"

Was it idle curiosity, or was Martha sussing out terri-
tory?

"On and off."

"Married?"

"Yes." What was she supposed to say? "No"? She still
felt married. Widowed. That was the correct and ugly
word. Black widow.

Martha nodded. "Thought so. Seen your wedding
ring."

Sandra prided herself on being honest but felt she was
slipping. Still, what did it matter? History had little to do
with facts. And she didn't owe this woman anything.

"Coffee?"

"Do you have tea?"

"Certainly." She made a pot and set tea and mugs on
the place mat in the middle of the table. "And here's your
sandwich." Golden triangles on a white plate, a sprig of
parsley.

"Very pretty. Thank you." Martha took a big bite.
The steaming mouthful came out as fast as it went in.

"Ouch. Sorry. Too hot!" Martha was fanning her face
with her mouth open, trying to cool her tongue.

"Would you like some water?"

"No, no, it's all right. Serves me right for being
greedy. Bit hungry. Haven't eaten since breakfast."

"How's that?"

"Well, I went to the hospital this morning, and there's the poor old bugger in one of those gowns with his bum hanging out because he didn't have any undies or jarmies."

"What did you say his name was?"

Martha laughed. "I don't know, really. It's either Clifford or Cliff Ford, which sounds silly. He talks funny sometimes. But he wasn't saying. Some people don't like to be pinned down. Anyway, I went and bought him this gear, but it used up all my cash. Then after I took it to him, I went home for a while, but I didn't have time to eat because I wanted to finish something for you."

Sandra did not know how to respond to such a comment, so she asked a question.

"How did you get here, with no money?"

"Multitrip ticket. You get ten bus trips. It's cheaper that way. But I must stop magging—I have to get the bus back. Just came to give you this." She unzipped the top of the large red, white and blue plastic bag and took out a cotton shopping bag with a supermarket brand emblazoned on one side. Whatever was in it was light and insubstantial.

"To say thank you for helping yesterday. I didn't know what to do next, and you came along like an angel in disguise."

Sandra peered into the bag. It looked like a mass of

silver fairy floss. Martha opened her sandwich and blew on it.

"Take it out. It's bigger than it looks."

It was a scarf—no, a shawl, light as air, but warm.

"It's beautiful!" The fabric was soft and springy, re-silient.

"Angora, very fine. Lovely stuff. Fits through a wed-ding ring."

Sandra caught the shawl in a tight circle between thumb and forefinger, and saw that it would.

"But there's no need. I didn't do anything. You're the one who looked after him. You're the one who should be getting gifts."

"Couldn't do it on my own, sweet pea. You had the mobile. It's OK. I want you to have it. Didn't cost much. Made it myself." Martha looked around. "It's a pretty house here, but it's cold. I reckon you need it."

Martha looked at her watch, stood with the last bite of the sandwich in her hand, and went to her line of lug-gage.

"Sorry. Got to run. Don't want to miss the bus back."

CLIFF left the hospital, walked down the long mile of Pulteney Street to South Terrace and crossed over into the South Parklands. The doctors hadn't finished the tests, but he was leaving, he was out of there. All that air condition-ing was enough to make you sick. He took his clasp knife from his pocket, cut the plastic name band from his wrist and dropped it into the bin.

It must have rained; the new grass looked fresh. There was a chill in the air, although the day was sunny. The buds were swelling on the trees. A few more nights in that hospital would have killed him. All the same, he was getting too old to sleep out, and in the next year or two he'd have to find a place that offered a little more comfort, somewhere dry, where the rain didn't run down his neck. But he'd be all right until next winter at least. Just now he needed some fresh air, a night or two under the starry bright, to get the thick hospital breath out of his lungs. Too many walls, too many bodies too close, and nothing to look at except concrete and bricks or the ugly old bloke opposite.

The hospitals did their best for you, same as the Salvation Army. He had a lot of time for the Salvos. It was good to wake up in a dry bed.

Cliff kept clear of the playground. He knew that the young mothers perceived him wrongly, an old scruff, maybe a paedophile, lurking around their children. He kept his clothes fairly clean, but he didn't shave too often. He liked to watch the kids playing, listen to their shouts and laughter, see how they overcame their little fears to go down the high slide. He liked kids, enjoyed their freedom and spontaneity. But he knew that to parents he looked dangerous; he had seen the distaste, the caution, on their faces. The older women talked to him sometimes, grand-mothers who had lived long enough not to be afraid, but some of the young ones were aggressively fearful, like bitches with pups.

Cliff crossed the Parklands, then the six lanes of Greenhill Road, and made his way down Porter Street, past the corner of Muggs Hill Road, where the church had free coffee on Sunday mornings. Near the end of Porter Street he turned left into the grassy path at the edge of the deep culvert. Not too many people walked along the culvert path, although it was a useful shortcut between two main roads. Most people preferred the open street. Every now and then the path was punctuated by yapping dogs stuck behind the high fences of their boring backyards, but for the most part it was quiet, and the dogs minded their own business. Wattlebirds nested in the bottlebrush, and in summer bright green parrots did regular checks for fruit and almonds.

He was going back to a spot he'd used before. It was between two sheds, well screened by a banana passionfruit vine gone berserk. You had to cross the culvert to get to it, two metres down and two metres up again. Once, a couple of years ago, there had been a storm upstream, and when Cliff woke up, the water was racing fast, a couple of metres from where he slept. It was as high as his neck, too danger-ous to cross, so he had to stay holed up in his cubby. He didn't fancy being swept into the tunnel where the culvert swung under the road. It was five or six hours before the flood subsided, and all he'd had to eat was a couple of oranges, filched earlier from a tree hanging over a fence.

It was a summer hideout, but it could take the occasional rain. He even had a roof now, a few sheets of galvanized iron that he inspected regularly for redback spiders. The area was full of orderly Greek and Italian gardens and well-oiled gates. A few people had put locks on their gates, but Cliff knew the friendly gardeners who let him pick a tomato or two. The locals knew where he camped and left him alone. He used his sister's address for things like Medicare, though he rarely slept at her house. He had no real need to forage, but it was more fun to rely on whatever life and goodness handed out. And if he did get stuck, the automatic teller had new money in it every fortnight, like eggs in a hen's nest. His wants were simple: he could buy clothes at op shops, day-old bread half price from the baker, a bottle of cheap port at the pub, and still have enough left over for a scratchie or two.

Cliff swung down into the culvert, using his familiar footholds, and up the other side, feeling stiff from too long in bed. His legs still worked, at any rate, though he was tired after the long walk, and he still had a scab on the side of his face after his fall in the Mall. His cubby was as good as ever. The last hard-rubbish day had provided a decent carpet, an armchair and a mattress. A piece of canvas had flapped loose. He rested for a while, then set about making repairs.

The following afternoon he walked down the culvert

a mile or so and pressed the doorbell of his sister's house. A short, stout woman opened it and smiled.

"Hello, Joyce."

"Hello, little brother," she said, giving him a hug. "Haven't seen you for a while. What have you been up to?"

"Hospital."

"Hospital! Why didn't you let me know?"

"Didn't want to worry you. It was only a few days. How's your ticker, anyway?"

"No trouble. A bit tight sometimes."

"That lad of yours behaving himself?"

Joyce pursed her lips in mock disapproval.

"No. Too much like his uncle. He's hitched up to Sydney to see the sights. Says he'll get work up there. Giving me a breather, at any rate. You should have told me you were crook."

"You have enough on your plate."

"I'd like to know if my own brother's in hospital, all the same. What was it?"

"Had a fit. Seizure. Fell over in the Mall. Only a couple of nice ladies picked me up and looked after me, and now I've got a girlfriend."

"No!"

"She's not really my girlfriend. But she's nice, Joyce. Real clever. Knits amazing patterns. She came to the hospital a couple of times and sat by my bed. Brought me pyjamas and undies and all." Cliff suddenly remembered he had left the pyjamas at the hospital. "So she must like me a bit."

"Don't get your hopes up. Where are you living now?"

"Back of Porter Street." He was always vague with Joyce. "Sort of a sleep-out."

"Cup of tea?"

"Won't say no." Joyce put the kettle on, took down the cake tin, got out cups and saucers. Cliff saw that her hands were knobbier than ever. She made real tea, in a teapot, and set it on the table between them.

"What's this about seizures, Cliff?"

"Epilepsy, maybe."

"What happened?"

"Just blacked out. I was looking in a shop window, and that's all I remember. Hit my face, see? Then this Martha comes along and tries to help, but she was all on her own, no one else would do anything. Then this other bird—I haven't met her, but Martha said her name's *Sahndra*," Cliff made a face, "rather posh—comes along and has a mobile and calls an ambulance. Nobody else wanted to help. Probably thought I was drunk."

"It does happen."

"Not to me, at any rate. Haven't had a drink for a long time. Can't get a port in hospital! Now, while I'm here, got anything you need done?"

Joyce had a big daisy root to grub out. It took Cliff

quite a while, and he needed a couple of rests, but it gave him great satisfaction to tear it out of the earth at last.

Before Cliff left, Joyce loaded him up with a cake, a bag of apples and a loaf of homemade bread. He'd be right for a couple of days with that lot.

UNDER the framed feathers, Sandra was sleeping. She could hear a cello. She knew this music, the introduction to Weber's *Invitation to the Dance*, orchestrated by Berlioz, 1841. She felt the ribbon laces of her pink shoes firmly around her ankles, the stiffened net of the tutu brushing at her elbows. There were feathers in her hair. She was ready and waiting, poised in the wings for her grand entrance, but she couldn't remember the story. Was it a wedding or a funeral? Jack was out there, dancing his solo, strong calf muscles filling out his white tights, arms in a graceful hoop above his head. He thrust a hand toward her in a gesture of longing: only a few more bars and it would be her moment. Jack would take her hand.

There was a story she couldn't remember, but it would come, she knew, with the first point of her toe, the first step. The invitation was so tender, so courteous. In a moment the music would course through her, strong and inevitable. She would lift her body to it and be carried along until—how did it end? She couldn't remember. She would have to give herself to the music to find out. The waltz began, and here came Jack, whirling faster and faster, smiling at her, young and handsome, leaner than she remembered, looking at her, Sandra, the fixed point for every spin. He flew away and circled back again, always looking for her. Now he was beckoning.

No, this was wrong. He was supposed to come and get her, take her hand and lead her out. He was calling her but not touching her; he wasn't helping her through the transition. When he took her hand she would remember the steps—she needed his strong fingers and that firm, steadying hand on her back. And the waltz was way too fast. She went cold with panic.

Jack danced further and further away, the stage grew bigger and bigger. She was still in the wings. Her tutu was white china, her shoes were little glass slippers. She was frozen, an ice sculpture.

Jack was far, far away on the other side, getting smaller and smaller, disappearing into the opposite wings. The music and the panic swelled together in a grand crescendo, then cut to sudden silence.

It was getting light. Sandra got up with a dry throat and, feeling slightly dizzy, made her way to the bathroom. On the way back she saw Martha's shawl hanging on the back of the chair. She drew the shawl over her upper body and cocooned herself under the bedclothes. It was warm and soft against her skin, just right.

MARTHA needed a break. She had finished the tea cosy

and the toilet-roll holder and was now knitting a fancy pair of socks for Cliff in a slipstitch mosaic, fluorescent green on black. Martha liked knitting socks; they were very satisfying. Big enough for experiments but small enough to finish quickly. She'd never made two pairs alike.

She'd been knitting for three days solid and the socks were nearly done, with no mistakes. But if she didn't have a rest now she'd soon start making them. The walls of her flat had started to feel like those of a hospital, and Martha knew the best cure for that was absence. She had some vague idea of going to the Botanic Garden, but mainly she wanted to get out of the flat and do something different for a change.

She heaved herself and her bags onto the bus to the city and took herself for a walk down North Terrace. Outside the Art Gallery was a banner advertising an international exhibition of fashion lace. After a good look at the notices to make sure it was free, Martha tucked her small leather purse into her pocket where she could keep one hand on it and left her luggage at the cloakroom. The man in uniform looked rather distastefully at the bags, which had to be heaved over the counter.

The lace exhibition was toward the back of the gallery. No staff were in the vicinity, but Martha took note of the security cameras and felt comforted.

Rounding the corner into the exhibition, Martha was startled by a tall black man in a white shirt standing directly in front of her, his legs wide, arms across his chest, each hand tucked into the opposite sleeve of his white shirt. He was so tall that she didn't look into his face, and besides, her attention caught on his shirt, which he wore loosely over his bare chest and black trousers. The top part had a mottled density, like ice on a river, with a hint of deep, dark water rushing beneath. The lower half, covering his midriff and hips, had been topstitched into triangles, and the triangles themselves had been cut out, so the contrast of his black skin beneath the white was stark and unmitigated. The bottom of the garment was jaggedly uneven.

Martha realised suddenly that this was a kind of lace, that here was a man wearing lace — and a big black man at that. She raised her eyes. Both he and the garment were beautiful.

"Excuse me, ma'am," he said, speaking to her politely in an American accent. He pointed behind her. "The guy over there is wanting to take my picture." Martha turned around and saw a photographer behind her, with bags as big as her own. He was opening silvery white umbrellas and fussing around with cameras and tripods.

"Do I have to leave?" she said. "I only just got here."

"We're nearly done," he said. "You can sit over there and watch if you like." He indicated a solitary chair against the far wall.

"Can I just—?" Martha extended one hand toward

the white stuff on his body.

"Sure. Go ahead."

She fingered the white fabric, felt the texture of fills and spaces, saw the ripple of the black muscled river beneath. Behind her the photographer grunted.

"Thank you," she said, looking up again into the man's generous face, and reached to smooth a wrinkle below his shoulder. But it wasn't a wrinkle, it was a gathering of whiteness, like a vein in marble. Underneath the soft fabric his arm was as solid as rock.

"You're welcome, ma'am," he said.

From her hard-backed chair Martha watched the final stages of the photo shoot. The photographer, she saw from his directions, was at pains to contrast the filmy fabric with the muscular man. And the man, she could see, was an artist himself and used to being photographed; he moved and smiled and simmered on cue, with such fine control that even the smallest movement created a subtle but noticeable change.

Ten minutes later Martha entered the main display. She had never seen such garments. Plastic bags knitted into dresses, a sun-yellow raincoat punched in a pattern the notice called "binary"—something to do with computers—a cloak made from handmade paper, a felt hat with bits of knitting wool laid flat in the felt like squashed coloured worms. There was a glass dress, too, made of thousands and thousands of beads. It was shimmering shiny and not very modest, but it was beautiful, hard and bright and beautiful. It was difficult to imagine a soft human body wearing an uncomfortable dress like that, but maybe it was just for looking and not wearing. Though that black man had been wearing one of these creations, the thick white lace spread over him like a second, holey skin, with teasing peepholes to the rocky forearms beneath. Black and white and beautiful, and good to touch, too. It must have been a natural fibre. His voice was kind. Maybe if you wore beautiful, comfy clothes it made you kind as well.

But this glass dress, this was a dress for a woman with a cutting voice and a snapping handbag, someone who ordered people around so they wouldn't see who she was. A dress for a woman who was always holding in a shriek but would let out only bits at a time, slivers of misery from behind those tight glass beads.

At the bus stop Martha waited, staring at a sparrow hopping about, her mind busy elsewhere. After Sandra's shawl she had started knitting the green and black socks for Cliff, something quick and simple, while she waited for clarity regarding her next large project. She could feel the idea coming now, nudging deep down between her belly and her heart, something beautiful and soft, something for love and joy and dancing. Martha's hand swept downward in a slow flourish with no regard for anyone watching, something that would *drape*, have a touch of—she searched for the word—*splendour*, that was it. A touch of *splendour.* She had better hurry up and finish those socks.

MARTHA had been home only a couple of minutes when she heard a knock at the front door. There stood Cliff holding a bunch of jonquils. They were not wrapped.

"For you," he said, "to say thanks for looking after me."

"Why, thank you, Mr Ford," said Martha with the suggestion of a curtsy. "That's very kind. Did they grow in your garden?"

"More or less," said Cliff.

"But how did you know where I lived?" asked Martha.

"I was out and about," said Cliff. "Saw you when you got off the bus. I yelled out, but you didn't hear, and it's taken me this long to catch up."

"So how did you have time to pick jonquils?"

"Just call me Mr Magic."

Martha laughed.

"Well, come in, Mr Magic, and have a nice fresh muffin." She led the way through to her little kitchen. "But don't go getting ideas. A muffin is all you're going to get. Well, maybe two muffins."

IT WAS raining, and the rush-hour traffic moved cautiously, but even so Sandra missed the turn to the church where she had agreed to meet Kate. She and Jack had been there once, to a candlelit Christmas service, invited by

Kate and Tony before Jack's illness, but in the confusion of bright headlights streaming on wet roads she overshot the turn. Sandra and Kate had arranged to have dinner after Kate's interview with a prospective new cleaner for the church. Kate was always doing some kind of volunteer job.

When Sandra arrived, it was past five-thirty. The lights were on above the side door into the office area, and warmth and light seemed a better option than sitting in a cold car. She picked her way across the flat-sheeted puddles, past the rose garden to the blue door. It was slightly ajar and she pushed her way in.

The church was old bluestone, but the office area, which Sandra now saw for the first time, surprised her with its array of high-tech equipment. Sandra had always associated churches with a certain fustiness that proclaimed their irrelevance. The reception area was carpeted and welcoming, the wall bright with a panel of children's paintings. Further down she could hear voices; the interview must still be in process. The paintings were full of arks and animals and varied interpretations of Noah, including one that showed him waving a beer bottle and looking decidedly tipsy.

She felt a sudden draft of cold air as someone else came in from outside. Sandra turned to see a tallish man, ill dressed, middle-aged, needing a shave, but striding confidently into this alien space. He nodded to Sandra, crossed the room, tapped on the door at the other end and disappeared behind it. The voices became more animated, and Sandra strained to hear, but she couldn't make anything out. A few minutes later the man came back.

"G'day," he said and extended his hand, at the same time giving Sandra's tailored jacket a quick once-over. "Nice to meet you. Have you come about the cleaning job?"

"No, I'm a friend of Kate Linkett's. I'm meeting her here." Sandra looked the man up and down in return. His trousers were a little short and he was wearing odd socks, a detail that tweaked at her memory, though she wasn't sure why.

"Oh, Kate. She's a good one, she is."

Sandra nodded, not sure what "good" meant in this context. The man was in no hurry to go.

"What about you?" asked Sandra, also curious. "Are you here for an interview?"

"No way!" The man laughed. "Wouldn't suit me. I like to be outside. Just came to put in a good word for me girlfriend."

The voices were louder, and the door was opening. They turned toward it to see a woman backing out with three large bags. Sandra recognised the bags before she saw the woman's face.

"Hello, Martha."

Martha looked up in surprise.

"Dr Fildes?"

"Oh, please, call me Sandra."

Martha looked mystified. "You don't want to be a cleaner, do you?"

"No." Sandra laughed.

"Oh." Martha paused and then smiled. "But you come to this church."

Sandra shook her head. "No, not me. I'm a friend of Kate's, who's helping with the interviews. We're going out for dinner." Kate had still not appeared.

"I come to this church, though," said the scruffy man. He turned to Martha. "How did you go?"

"All right, I think. Wait and see."

"This is your boyfriend?" Sandra asked Martha.

"Cliff? No way!" Martha laughed. The man reddened beneath his stubble as Sandra stared at him.

"Cliff?" asked Sandra. "Are you *that* Cliff?"

Martha laughed again.

"Yes, the same one! Cliff, do you know who this lady is?"

Cliff shook his head.

"The one with the mobile. The one who called the ambulance the day you collapsed in the Mall. It's her, Sandra. You know, I told you, she called the ambulance, and then I went to see her and she gave me a toasted cheese sandwich for tea."

"Ah," said Cliff. "That one. I see." He paused, then shook Sandra's hand again, and bowed over it. "Thank you, madam. Thank you very much. Very kind of you indeed." He was still shaking her hand.

"Are you all right now?" asked Sandra, pulling back.

"Yes, yes. Nothing much. Just banged my head, I think. Knocked all the sense out of it."

"Excuse me, have to catch my bus," said Martha.

"I'll help you," said Cliff, reaching for the brown suitcase.

"No, thanks, I'm used to it," said Martha, quickly grabbing the handle. "It balances me. If I don't carry them myself I feel awkward."

"Well, I'll just see you to the bus stop," said Cliff. He reminded Sandra of a labrador puppy.

Martha sighed. "OK. Come on, then." Her hands were full, so she lifted an elbow to Sandra in a parody of a wave. "Nice to meet you again, Sandra. Might see you round." They made their way out the door. Cliff ignored Sandra; his attention was focused on Martha.

Kate suddenly appeared. "Have they gone already?"

"Martha had to catch a bus."

"Oh, I meant to say goodbye. Never mind, I'll talk to her later. Just hang on a moment while I get my bag."

"How old is this building?" asked Sandra when Kate came back.

"Can't tell you exactly, though it had its centenary before we arrived. Do you want to see the rest of it? The church is just through there."

Kate led her into an open space with a lofty ceiling

and stained glass windows.

"We had it modernised a few years ago. These are new seats. The old ones were designed to keep you bolt upright. It's a great space now, very flexible. We have dinners here sometimes. And through here"—Kate led Sandra into a side lobby, switching on lights as they went, then opened another door—"is the old church hall."

"What a wonderful floor!" They were standing at the edge of an expanse of polished wooden floorboards. Sandra suddenly remembered herself as a child, tap-dancing across the church hall on Saturday mornings, delighting in the rhythmic echo of her two strong feet. She had sat in that same church hall for Sunday school, where her parents had sent her for a couple of years to broaden her education, while they stayed home and did the gardening. She remembered little of Sunday school, other than the story of King David "dancing before the Lord with all his might" before the returning ark of the covenant, and how his wife had despised him for it.

"Well, yes," said Kate. "The floor looks great, but the acoustics are terrible. The kids love to run on it. We'll probably carpet it one day, but it's used as a dance studio during the week. Well, that's it. Let's go. I'm hungry. Interviews are hard work."

In the car, Sandra told Kate about the connection with Cliff and Martha and the conversation they'd just had. "You church people sure attract some weirdos."

"So do you," retorted Kate. "You met them in the Mall all by yourself."

"But Cliff? Aren't you scared he'll run off with the collection?"

"He might." Kate shrugged.

"Did you give Martha the job?"

"Yes, for a trial period. The others were worried about what Martha might carry off in those bags. I think she'll be fine. Doesn't strike me as the thieving sort."

"And if either of them *does* run off with the silver?"

"It's only money, Sandra. Besides, we've got insurance."

MARTHA decided she should attend at least one service at the church to have a good look at her clients. When Kate had shown her around, she had seen a mess of crumbs in one corner that didn't make sense. She came in early, parked her bags on the floor at the wall end of the pew and sat down beside them. Ah, that was it. Tea and coffee were served beforehand, with plain sugary biscuits. Well, any church that offered you a coffee on arrival was better than most.

Sandra was also in church that morning. Kate's husband, Tony, was away on a business trip. Sandra had spent the evening at Kate's with art-house videos and good wine and then stayed the night. In the morning it seemed impolite to refuse Kate's invitation to attend church. They were a few minutes early. Sandra watched the congregation assemble, noted the excitement of the children, the elderly clustering under the wall-mounted heaters. And there was Martha again, a few pews forward and hard up against the wall.

"I didn't think Martha came to church," said Sandra to Kate.

"Never has before. I'll just go and say hello."

Sandra envied Kate's ease with people. She watched her sit down next to Martha and exchange a few words. Martha looked around at Sandra and nodded, then shook her head at Kate. They talked some more and Kate came back to sit by Sandra.

"What did you say to her?"

"I invited her to sit back here with us, but she said her bags would take up too much room. She's a funny bird. But she's coming back for lunch. I hope you don't mind."

Inwardly Sandra groaned. She opened the church bulletin and concentrated on the prayer list. Did people mind, she wondered, having their names listed to be prayed for? Evidently not. What would Jack have made of it? *Pray for Jack Fildes, starting chemotherapy this week. And for his wife, Sandra, in her Great Dark.* No, there was nothing as personal as that. But what if Kate had offered to pray? It might feel nice to be wrapped in someone's prayer. Not in their presence of course, no, God forbid, but to be prayed for *in absentia*, she could cope with that. Only Kate had never asked. Perhaps she prayed without permission.

Martha, unabashedly looking about the church, noticed that Sandra did not have a husband with her, even though she had said she was married and wore a ring. Sandra was short, but her friend Kate was tall, thin around the shoulders, with a round face that seemed at odds with her angular body. She was wearing an interestingly patterned jacket that Martha felt sure was rayon, but she would have to touch it to be certain. Martha was curious about Sandra and had eagerly accepted the invitation to lunch.

After church they sat together in Kate's kitchen while Kate finished preparing the salad. She told Martha she had a husband, Tony, who was away because of work, and a twelve-year-old son, Jeremy, who was at a friend's place.

Martha's bags were by the wall where she could keep an eye on them. She watched Sandra set the table. Sandra obviously knew her way around this kitchen, was familiar with the cupboards. She'd said she was married, but she never mentioned her husband. Perhaps, like Kate's, he was away with work. Perhaps the two men had gone together.

"Was that Tony who rang this morning?" Sandra asked Kate. The ringing phone had woken her.

"Yes. He's homesick. It's a long stretch this time. Seven weeks. I really miss him." She looked at Sandra suddenly, furtively, as though embarrassed, but Sandra had her head down over the soup spoons. Kate turned to Martha. "My husband travels a lot in his job. He's in Vancouver at the moment. Anyway, what about you, Martha? Do you have a partner?"

"No."

Martha was still watching Sandra. Something fishy was going on here.

"What about before now?" asked Kate brightly.

"Well, yes," said Martha. "I was married once. When I was seventeen I married the boy down the road."

"What happened to him?" asked Kate. "Did it work out? That's very young."

"No, we were happy all right. But he's dead now." Martha was talking to Kate but watching Sandra, and saw the small pause as she laid out the spoons.

"What happened?" Kate asked.

"Give her a break," said Sandra. "What is this, the Church Interrogation Society?"

"I don't mind," said Martha mildly. "It was a long time ago. He was a lovely boy. Twenty years old and beautiful. Big muscles, with a nice rose tat on one shoulder. Accident."

Kate brought the soup to the table.

"Anyway," asked Martha. "What's your bloke up to, Sandra?"

Martha could not interpret Kate's sudden alertness.

"Wish I knew," Sandra said, and laughed tightly. "He's dead too. Ten months ago. Cancer."

Ah, now Martha understood.

"But you still feel married, don't you?" she said. "It takes a long time to get over it."

To SAVE Martha the trouble of catching a bus into the city and out again, Sandra offered her a ride home. It had been a pleasant afternoon after all, and in the end Martha had fitted in well enough: even if she wasn't quite their sort, at least she had a creative turn of phrase that made them laugh. And Sandra was pleased with herself for making the effort, putting her grief aside for a while and managing to relate to someone not only new but different from her usual companions. She had made a good fist of it for once.

Martha too had seemed to enjoy herself, taking out her knitting after lunch, deftly weaving in the many-coloured strands of a complicated sock. Kate had fetched her quilting basket and sewn a few pieces together for a patchwork sampler. Sandra, not to be outdone, secured some dangerously loose buttons on her jacket. The three women sat peaceably through an afternoon they punctuated at intervals with cups of coffee.

At one point they discussed knitting, the making of Sandra's shawl, and Sandra's work teaching textile history and theory. Sandra offered a few pieces from her current research, about the resurgence of home crafts in the wake of the terrorist attacks on the World Trade Center, and the trend toward complex yarns rather than complex stitches as a new generation learnt to knit. Interest in knitting was cyclical, Martha said, like yo-yos, only the craze lasted several years instead of a few weeks. Kate said she always had to be doing something with her hands, that some life force at work in the creative act kept her sane.

WHEN they arrived at Martha's place, Martha invited Sandra in to show her a wartime pattern book. Turning from the small porch area into Martha's living room, Sandra was startled by the head and forequarters of a life-sized orange horse. At first, absurdly, she had thought it was a real horse—the shape had loomed at her from beside the closed curtains of Martha's darkened living room.

Martha pushed the curtains back and Sandra saw that the head and withers were suspended from the ceiling by transparent fishing line, and the whole was made of knitted stocking stitch. Only the front was complete, but that was well made with fine attention to detail; something in the blaze under the woolly forelock, the flare of the nostrils, and the angle of the ears cocked to the front was focused and endearing. Anyone standing in front of it had that horse's full attention. The sheer size—thirteen hands, at least, thought Sandra automatically—was impressive.

"Do you like old Mickey?" asked Martha.

"He's wonderful."

"A bit of fun in my spare time. Just knit a new bit here and there every now and again. Starting on the saddle blanket next."

"I never thought you'd keep a horse in your flat!"

"Well, there you go. You can't always tell by appearances. I didn't know you had a swimming pool till you mentioned it today. You can't tell from the front." Martha stepped back and looked critically at the horse.

"Don't know what I'll do with him when he's finished. He's already getting too big, and he's not half done yet."

"What's he for? Anything special?"

"Nup. Just a bit of fun and games. Keeps me amused when I'm not doing tea cosies and socks." A tea cosy, Sandra thought, must be a tedious bit of nonsense for such an artist.

"Have you ever done anything like this before?"

"No."

"You could knit a whole zoo! Or a farmyard."

"I don't think so. One animal is enough. I just wanted to see if I could do it. It's not that hard. See, I'm working from these." Martha showed Sandra photocopies of anatomical drawings. "Got them from a vet book in the library. Helps me get the proportions right, because it's hard to remember. I had a horse once, but I still need these drawings for instructions. You forget how the muscles work."

"I wouldn't call those instructions."

"They're the best sort. Pictures to follow."

"But there's no words, no rules. How can you do it

with no words? How do you know how many stitches to cast on?"

"You just try it out. If it doesn't work, you try a different way. If you have words, you have rules, and rules have to be obeyed. But this way, when you look at the drawings, the pattern gets into your heart somehow. The rules are still there but you hardly notice. It's much bigger and better than rules!"

Sandra tried to take it in: knitting without rules. No, beyond rules—that's what Martha was saying.

"What are you going to do with him?"

"I dunno. Would you like him?"

"No, no. I mean, I couldn't. But he should be shown off somewhere. He's so handsome, so unusual. It's definitely a 'he'?"

"Yes, he's Mickey. Poor old Mick. The first Mickey is just worm food now, down the bottom paddock."

"Are you going to do the whole thing? The tail and everything?"

"Probably. Take me another six months though, maybe more. Meanwhile he's good company. Doesn't talk too much. I just fit him in around other stuff. Now come in here, and I'll find that pattern book."

They turned into a spare room that smelled like mothballs. It was like walking into a wool shop. Along one wall was a low honeycomb of triangular shelving, each one jewelled with balls of richly coloured wool: rose, amethyst, amber, jade, sapphire, opal, emerald, jet. Sandra couldn't help feeling she'd walked into some kind of adult playground. In one corner was a huge bag of orange yarn, the same colour as the horse, and next to it a large basket of unspun fleece and a spinning wheel. Silver cylinders — were they really jam tins? — bristled with knitting needles, and glass-topped pins were stuck in the back of a hand-knitted hedgehog. The walls were dense with pictures cut from calendars and magazines, each with a different theme. The wall opposite the window was filled with galaxies, stars, moons, a large solar system, photos of the earth and various planets taken from outer space. There were no rockets or spaceships. Next to a fiery nebula was an illustration Sandra recognized from an article in *Time* magazine about black holes.

On Sandra's left the wall was covered with pictures of leaves and trees, close-ups of daisies, orchids and roses, large rainforest landscapes of towering trees and matted ferns, here and there a gleaming beetle or a backlit scattering of seeds. Bright greens, secret shadow corners for tiny glowing fungi, echoes of flapping wings, bird song and the critching sound of cicadas. The wall throbbed with energy and growth.

The third wall was large with deserts and silence. Movement that must be measured in months and years and aeons, minimalist landscapes of sand dunes, moraines, flat red gibber plains, green ice, blinding snowfields, rock crevices, the crater of an extinct volcano. Behind her back Sandra felt the exuberant plants budding and bursting, pushing out fruit and flowers, while in front of her were silence, solitude, the bare whisper of wind.

Martha was flicking through folders in a large filing cabinet. Sandra was surprised by the number of files, more consistent with academic research. Her heart leapt.

"Are these all knitting files?"

"Mainly. But I also keep diaries and other things. Here you are." She held out an old knitting book, illustrated in black and white, with a man in army uniform on the front and the words 'Home Comforts for our Fine Brave Boys' in white copperplate cursive. Sandra accepted the thin pattern book, but her attention was on the filing drawer.

"Are these all patterns?"

"No, lots of things. But all to do with knitting." Martha took out another folder. "Look here. These are all pictures of knitters. They seem like old friends to me."

Sandra leafed through them. A gallery postcard of *The Sock Knitter*, a 1915 painting by Sydney artist Grace Cossington Smith; a black-and-white photo torn from a magazine, showing a large woman, cigarette dangling from her lips, sitting on a stool and knitting a straggling scarf; a colour photocopy from a textile-arts book of an 1869 painting by Bouguereau, *The Knitting Girl*. Here they were, representations of the knitter. Without her even asking.

"Martha, these are wonderful files! Do you have any more war patterns? I've been interested in textiles for years, but I haven't collected knitting patterns."

"A few, I think." Martha went on searching.

Sandra went home with five slim black-and-white pattern books, all more than fifty years old. Such an unexpected return.

THE following day the yarn sample cards Martha had ordered arrived in the mail. She made a cup of tea for her card-opening ceremony, then, using a fine knitting needle, opened all the envelopes. The blue and green silks were wonderful; the light from the window played over the lustrous fibres like water. But the cashmere was so soft.

Martha held the threads against her cheek and read aloud from the notes. "More warmth per weight than any other natural fibre in the world. Goats can take between four and six years to grow enough cashmere for one average jumper. The soft underfleece is gathered by hand-combing every spring. In the past most cashmere has come from Afghanistan, Iran, Outer Mongolia, India and China, but in the last decade or so Australia and New Zealand have begun producing their own."

The cashmere was beautiful but too soft, perhaps. The lambswool–cashmere blend might hold its shape better, but the wispy texture would lessen the effect of any patterning. And the yarn had to be fine. Two ends at most, knitted carefully together.

Martha needed a second cup of tea before she could decide. She would go for lambswool after all. She was more familiar with wool, how it handled and how to care for it, and the micron count was very similar to the cashmere. The untrained touch would hardly be aware of the difference, and practicality had to be considered.

Lambswool, then. And white. Yes, it had to be white. Pure as the driven snow.

SANDRA wasn't exactly sure why she had asked Martha about the patterns, though she knew it was connected to the article about Greek artefacts: an idea was forming in the back of her head, a collection or display. Something to demonstrate the intersection of language and women's work, or the development of metaphoric language — spinning a yarn, weaving a story, seamlessness. Stitching, embroidery, knitting, handcraft. Something like that.

At home she took the knitting patterns to her study. The first book, printed in 1945, had a matt black-and-white cover. The end of the war, then, with rationing still in place. Clothing coupons. Yes, just as she thought, the writing had a certain turn of phrase, a definitive language, slightly jingoistic. The language of genteel survival in the face of war.

Next was a women's pattern book from the same era.

Sandra looked at the copy on the front cover:

FOUR PRETTY KNITTEDS TO MAKE FOR YOURSELF

A lacy knit frock, the prettiest you've seen for some time
A sleeveless pullover with embossed motifs for the outdoor
 girl
A jumper in unusual bluebell design for the more mature
 woman
This time it's smart to wear your heart on your sleeve in
 this romantic fluffy cardigan adorned with interwoven
 hearts

She'd use it for next Wednesday's class and see what her students made of it. And she must remember to register for that textiles conference. Later, just before sleeping, Sandra suddenly thought of Martha's luggage. What could be so important that she needed to lug it around all the time? Those bags were heavy; Sandra had seen that it took a fair amount of effort to carry them. Perhaps she really was a bag lady who collected bottles and cans to supplement her income.

FRESH green leaves were sprouting from the trees, but it was still chilly. Sandra bought herself a small black coffee in the little café next to the supermarket and positioned herself by the window, where she would have the full benefit of the afternoon sun. It was Saturday, shopping day, but the shopping could wait till she had read the paper.

She was halfway through the book pages when a shadow fell across the table. Deep in an interview with a favorite author, she ignored it, but a finger tapping on the other side of the glass made her look up.

Outside on the pavement stood Martha and Cliff. Martha was motionless, two bags in one hand and the small suitcase in the other. Cliff tapped again with a brown finger. They were laughing. Sandra smiled uncertainly. Were they laughing at her?

Martha raised her eyebrows and pointed at Sandra's table. It was clear she was asking if they could join her. Martha would be all right, but Sandra could have done without Cliff. Oh well, she could excuse herself. She beckoned them in.

Cliff moved through the tables with surprising grace and sat down in the chair adjacent to Sandra's. Martha, encumbered by her bags, struggled to find passageway. One bag caught on the back of a chair and tipped it over. She righted it and apologised profusely to the smart young couple at the table. They smiled icily. When she sat down, Sandra saw that her eyes were full of tears.

"Can I get you both a coffee?"

Cliff inclined his head regally. "For this, good thanks, m'lady." Sandra wanted to laugh.

"Martha?"

"Oh, you don't need to," began Martha awkwardly, then said meekly, "Oh, yes, please, if you don't mind.

White with one."

Sandra ordered at the counter and went back to her seat. Martha still looked embarrassed. Cliff spoke first.

"Do you come here often?"

"Well, I come here to shop, but I don't often stop for coffee. What about you?"

"Not me. Just tagging along with Mattie here, who was wanting some wool. But they didn't have what she wanted, did they, Matt?"

Sandra couldn't figure Cliff out. He seemed a patchwork of roughness and gentility.

The coffee came. Sandra would have to stay a little longer to avoid seeming rude. Cliff put four spoons of sugar in his coffee and saw Sandra watching.

"Well, it's free, isn't it? Lots of calories. Just what I need." Cliff's skinny frame certainly didn't have calories to spare.

"What do you want the wool for, Martha?" asked Sandra.

"Not wool, cotton. To make a hat for summer. You know, those floppy ones, like a washing hat, to shade your face. I lost mine on the bus last year."

"Wouldn't it be cheaper to buy one?"

"Probably. But I make all my things, like in the old days. More environmentally friendly. No plastic packaging, no heavy transport from one side of the country to the other. I hand-sew some things. Slow work like that is soothing." Martha was talking fast, not quite at ease.

"You don't make everything by hand, surely?"

"Pretty much. It's very satisfying, making things from scratch. Fabric, needle, thread. Scissors. That's all you need."

"No machine?"

"Not now. I did once. A few years ago I used to spin and dye all my own wool too, but I stopped that. I like bright colours, and I like them colourfast. You can't do everything. But with sewing and knitting you can make most things. I buy my bras, though, and my shoes. That's about all."

"You don't really need them," said Cliff, grinning.

Martha looked quickly at Sandra.

"Behave yourself," she said. "Mind your manners. And weren't you going somewhere?"

Cliff looked surprised, then gulped the last of his coffee and stood up.

"Well, ladies, I'll leave you to it."

"What's with him?" said Sandra as they watched him cross the car park. "He's a bit strange, isn't he?"

"Oh, he's all right. That's just how he is. He reads, you know. He spends whole days in the library. And he's in love with me." She spoke matter-of-factly.

"Do you mind?"

Martha, more relaxed now, laughed out loud. "Mind? Why should I? It's a compliment. Look, don't touch, I told him."

"Did he try?"

"No, no. He's not creepy like that. He's honest and straightforward." She saw the doubting look on Sandra's face.

"He is. Trust me. He wouldn't hurt a fly. Got a heart of gold—you should hear him talk about his sister. Just doesn't care about money and houses like most people." There was a pause while Sandra tried to imagine such an existence.

"Martha, after your husband died, how was it?"

Martha looked her in the eye.

"It was terrible," she said. "We'd only been married a few months. I nearly went mad with it. In fact, I did go mad." She looked away.

"And then what?"

"I started knitting. And here I am."

"Are you still sad?"

"No. Just—" Martha paused.

Sandra waited. It was a good interview technique, she'd found. Hold the pause. Something useful usually came out.

"Just what, Martha?" She spoke very gently. Martha was still looking into the distance.

"You can't undo things. You can't go back. And all those things you did wrong, they just about kill you."

Sandra was disappointed. This wasn't relevant to the

line of inquiry. Martha laughed suddenly.

"So watch out, Sandra, I might still be a bit mad!"

"And children? Didn't you want children?"

"Yes, I did, but Manny died and then there wasn't anyone else. What about you?"

"Things don't always work out," said Sandra.

"No, not like we expect, anyway. And I wouldn't have been a very good mother."

"What makes you say that?"

"I just know, that's all. Thanks for the coffee, Sandra. I need to go now. I've got things to do."

September

MARTHA WAS an independent woman but was aware that other people often needed her. At the moment it was Cliff, and perhaps that tight little woman called Sandra needed her too. Certainly she had needed a warm shawl in that shivery house.

In the past it had mainly been professional people: social workers, doctors, a psychiatrist, even a lawyer. Now she mainly cared for friends and neighbors, like the Iraqi family two doors up, or Mary Sherbet next door, or anyone else who happened along. She had a generous heart and what she called a "double-jointed head", meaning she could simultaneously carry on a conversation and keep count of her knitting, which had been disconcerting for the lawyer.

As for the psychiatrist, he had wanted her to knit granny squares and had commissioned a rug. Martha had protested that granny squares were boring, but he had insisted. She must do something, he said, and she had once mentioned knitting. In the end she got better in spite of him.

Martha had a share-farming agreement with her brother, though times were hard on the farm. Thrifty and resourceful, she found she could manage well enough without drawing against her share of farm capital, but when her brother married, two women in the same kitchen proved impossible. Martha moved to her unit in Adelaide and began to knit in earnest, broadening her ideas by exploring galleries on weekends and finally landing the job knitting for the designer. It wasn't long before her garments were selling in Sydney and Melbourne.

The psychiatrist caused Martha more distress than even Manny's death, gradually eroding her self-confidence while purporting to do the opposite. In the years since hospital she wished she had been more robust and had stood up to him, demanding that he see *her* rather than a set of problematic quirks. It had taken Martha three unhappy years to realize what was happening and make her escape.

She wanted closure, so he got his granny squares, blacks and browns and greys, all neatly sewn together into a subversive knee rug full of slits, tucks, peaks, bobbles, twisted cords and openwork medallions, here and there missing an entire square. The young man didn't have enough knowledge to recognise art when he saw it, but Martha had a certain pleasure in charging him fifty dollars and saying goodbye. The wool had cost twenty, but never mind that. For good measure she made him a Christmas present, a balaclava without eye holes. He failed to see the joke.

But all that was long ago. Now other people needed her, and today it was Cliff needing company. He was interested in more than just her company, but Martha had told him firmly and politely that she wasn't interested. She wasn't closed to the idea, she said, but she wasn't one to go looking.

"You are very nice, Cliffy," she said. "But I don't think you're really my type. I'd like to be friends, though, if you can cope with that." He hadn't quite got the message yet, but he would sooner or later.

It was opening day for the Royal Adelaide Show. Cliff and Martha stood in the queue, excited as a couple of teenagers. It was good to get there early, said Martha, when everything was clean and sparkling and the salespeople were still smiling because their feet had not begun to hurt.

Martha took only twenty dollars, knowing that if she took more she'd spend it. Besides, the things she really cared about, like the animal nursery and the knitting displays, were free. Cliff had gone to the bank and taken out eighty dollars, but he'd blown seventy by lunchtime, throwing red balls down the open mouths of head-wagging clowns, tossing hoops at deceptively angled hooks, and shooting at ducks with cockeyed rifles. Martha steered them toward the hot-dog van so that Cliff would have something to eat before he spent the lot. She understood his total disregard for money. Cliff was not one to think about accumulating wealth or goods. He travelled light, he said, and all his goods could be rolled up in a blanket. Martha knew that he often gave money to street kids, to save them getting it by other means. As for his gambling, his pleasure was more in the anticipation than in the winning. If you had somewhere dry to sleep, clothes to wear, and occasional food, life was hunky-dory. He played the pokies a little, but he liked the horses and scratchies better. He had his own moral code—never borrow to bet— though he often ran out of cash well before pension day.

After lunch they had an argument about what to see next. Cliff wanted to see the cars and the farm machinery. His grandfather had been a farmer, and Cliff liked to think he had farming in his blood. Martha, who really did have farming in her blood, was far more interested in the knitting and embroidery. They decided to split up and meet later by the fountain at the front of the main hall.

But it was Cliff, on his way to the farm machinery, who found knitting first, though not the kind Martha sought. It was in the sales pavilion for electric appliances. At first he thought the strange machine was a musical instrument, but then he saw the threads of wool strung through shiny hooks and realised that the demonstrator, pushing a handle back and forth across the machine, was making fabric like Martha's knitting, which mysteriously emerged from underneath. He stood and watched, mesmerised by the steady rhythm.

"Interested in knitting machines?"

Ah. A knitting machine. He could see the pattern now, a complicated symmetry of several colours.

The demonstrator saw she would never make a sale here, but she had no other buyers, and he seemed genuinely interested in what she was doing. She smiled at him, which gave Cliff the courage to ask a question.

"How long does it take to do a row?"

"This long." Whoosh. The demonstrator laughed at the look on his face. "Quicker than the wife can do a row, hey?"

"I'm not married."

"Well, your girlfriend then. Why don't you buy her one?"

"I'd have to save up."

"Well, you save up then. And when you've got enough, you ring me. Here's my card."

Cliff patted the little pink card into his shirt pocket and buttoned the flap, then bowed to the woman, which made her laugh. Right. Time for the farm machinery.

MARTHA was lost among the flowers. She felt trapped in the long rows of white tablecloths, with their equally long rows of flowers in bottles and jars. She wanted to get to the knitting, but she couldn't seem to get past camellias and daffodils. She didn't want to waste this time alone, away from Cliff, a time when she could look at things she wanted to see, but she couldn't find her way out. She couldn't remember which direction to go in for the knitting, and whenever she got to a doorway she saw the wrong building outside, so she was forced back among flowers she didn't want to see: camellias perched unnaturally on plates like the bodiless heads of babies, rows of daffodils mocking her from their evenly spaced glass bottles, spiky cacti leering through their prickles, bonsai crouching, elegantly forlorn in their ceramic dishes of tiny gravel.

But then there were roses. Martha's racing heart slowed. Of all the flowers, these were the most comforting and familiar, the flowers her mother had nurtured between the house and the vegie patch, fenced from marauding cows.

Pink roses, red roses, yellow roses, roses blue and purple like bruises. Roses so dark they were almost black. Martha began to read the names. A large red rose with wide white stripes was called Hurdy Gurdy, just right for the show, and a wine-purple Old Port made her think briefly of Cliff. But it was the pink roses that caught her attention. Soft Celestial, with its heavenly name, the large pink plates of Echo, the shy blush double blooms of First

Love. Madame President was strongly pink, quite gorgeous, but the name made Martha laugh. That would be the day. A woman president for Australia.

And then she saw it, a rose called Martha, a generous, open-hearted rose, a delicate pink, but strong and clear, part of a display called Old Garden Varieties. She picked up a brochure and read slowly through the column until she found it.

> MARTHA: a sport of 'Zéphirine Drouhin'. Introduced in 1912. A climbing Bourbon. Grows up to 3 metres. Thornless. Vigorous, long-flowering, healthy. Perfumed. Not commonly found.

A rose called Martha. She could hardly believe it. But here it was in writing, in the middle of the Royal Adelaide Show. Martha. Not commonly found. Healthy and vigorous, and all those other things too.

THEY stayed until closing. Cliff stood aside to let Martha get on the bus. When she sat down, rugged up in her coat, he sat next to her. The seat was narrow, with a restraining bar at his thigh, so he had to sit close and squeeze Martha against the window. She sat with her hands crossed through the handles of her handbag. For once she had left her big bags at home.

Cliff felt like a king. He had insisted they stay for the fireworks, and Martha had loved them. She had clapped her hands in pleasure at each new explosion of colour. Martha had nice hands. Not like Sandra. When he shook hands with Sandra, it was like shaking hands with a doll. Her fingers were little and white, like icicles. Martha's fingers were thick and strong and warm, and the backs had only just started to freckle. It would be nice to hold one of those good hands, one of the hands that had helped him that day he fell in the street. He saw that Martha's watch was crooked and poked below her sleeve. He could just take hold of that hand and turn her wrist to see the time, then pull her hand down into the warmth between their bodies and hold it there all the way home. She was thinking about something else, though. She appeared to be quite distracted

"What's the time, Mattie?" he asked, taking her wrist and tilting the watch face so he could see it. He couldn't read it; the light was poor, and numbers seemed to be smaller these days. He kept holding her hand, but she pulled it away.

"You don't want a girlfriend, Cliff," she said. "You want a mother."

"No, I don't," he said. "A mother wouldn't keep me warm at night."

"If that's what you want, I'll make you some bed socks. I'll get right on it. Look, I only ever had one good boyfriend, and I married him. One's enough. The first one was such a good fit I don't want another."

Bugger, thought Cliff. Gambled and lost. But maybe

it was just as well. If Martha had responded differently, he might have found he wasn't up to it. Some things just didn't work as well as they used to.

SANDRA, needing a haircut before she went to the conference, rang the salon in the big department store across from the university. They could fit her in with Perron during her lunch break. Perron. What kind of a name was that? She remembered a Perron from when she was in Year 10. When they were working on *papier mâché* puppets, he had jerked his finger in and out of the gluey puppet head to make sucking noises. Her last haircut had been a disaster, the final in a series of not very good cuts. Until now she had not had the energy to change. She needed someone new, so she asked the office staff at work. In her department there was an unspoken understanding that personal matters—home and family, partners, ageing parents—were not discussed.

Perron was pushing forty, dark roots showing in bleached hair, and an odd touch of pink over one ear. He had the beginnings of a potbelly; his clothes were all black with sleeves half-mast on hairy golden arms. He walked around the salon like a cockerel in charge of hens.

Sandra flicked through the magazines as she waited for him. They were full of clothes and hair, no writing except for one-line captions for the images or slabs of advertising inadequately disguised as articles.

Perron came for her. Charming. She mutely followed

him to the mirror and sat down. Close up he looked older than she had first thought. He returned her gaze in the mirror, looking into her eyes. He ran his hands around the line of her hair.

"What would you like?"

"Something smarter. I've just sacked the old hairdresser for incompetence." She grimaced. "So see what you can do. Open slather."

He pulled at the tufts of hair behind her ears. "Do you still want this to show at the front?"

"I don't care, whatever you think best. I believe in giving a new hairdresser a fair go."

"Come over here to the basin."

Sandra was surprised. She had expected that someone lower in the pecking order would do the wash. He threw the black cape around her, gave her an anonymous body, tipped her head back to the basin. He took his time getting the water hot. When it came it was just right, coursing hard and strong against her scalp.

He had good hands, firm in the lathering. They discussed their work briefly.

He had been an oyster shucker and a waiter, silver service. But he wasn't a talker, not a yabberer like the last insufferable woman. This was a relief to Sandra, who preferred silence.

"Do you want a treatment?" asked Perron.

"No thanks."

The conditioner, smooth and silky. Perron's thigh pushed against her shoulder, his hands pushing and pulling at her scalp, around the crown, behind the temples and ears, the nape of her neck, where she stored tension. Head massage, standard treatment, but he was good, very good. She wanted to close her eyes and relax, but that was too submissive somehow, an admission of intimacy she didn't want. Was it a turn-on for him, rubbing women's heads? Or was it a power trip, watching them relax under his hands? She didn't know whether to close her eyes or leave them open. She settled for half closed.

Why was she always alert, on guard?

His leg against her shoulder was—what? Comforting? Stimulating? Bloody hell, Sandra, she said to herself, shut up and just enjoy it.

But she knew what it was: skin hunger. She wanted touch—craved touch, skin on skin, smoothing and easing. Not sex. She wanted massage without mess, without the work and the implications, to resolve the terrible tightness in her back and buttocks. Her right leg had been giving her trouble, the muscles around the hip needed stretching. The physiotherapist had suggested massage or rolling on a tennis ball. The tennis ball was hopeless. She was getting old, her body was betraying her.

It would be good to lie in the sun and soak in warmth. It had been a long winter.

Perron was cutting now, snippety snip, careful, not too much at the beginning.

She hadn't put on her makeup properly. Her forehead was white under the hair, and now more of it showed. In this light the grey hair didn't look too bad.

Perron rubbed three different products into her hair. He didn't ask permission. She didn't protest.

On one side her hair grew thicker. He saw it and took to it with thinning scissors. He took time with the blowing and settling, then twisted the hand mirror behind her so she could see the back.

"Good. Thanks." She was very pleased with it but wouldn't flatter him. "I'll give it a couple of days. You can never tell first up."

"It's a good cut," he said. "And you've got good hair. Strong, and plenty of it." She signed the Visa slip without checking the amount.

Back at work the office staff complimented her. None of the teaching staff appeared to notice.

ON PENSION day Cliff walked to the newsagent, counting his steps on the way. Three thousand and forty-two. If it was more than four thousand steps to the newsagent *and* if he put his left foot into the shop first, he would buy a five-dollar scratchie instead of a two-dollar one. No, no, if he saw three wattlebirds before he got to the end of the street, he would get a five-dollar scratchie. It was nearly the end of the street. Make that one wattlebird. No, that was no good. If he saw a red car between here and the newsagent, then he would get one, no cheating.

No red cars. Where were they all? What the heck. He'd get a five-dollar one anyway. Call it a treat for the beginning of spring.

Nothing. Another dud. His luck had better change soon, or he'd go bananas.

MARTHA lugged the vacuum cleaner into the church, where the sunlight was washing through the stained glass windows with the memorial plaques underneath saying who had died in the war. It was so long ago, and people were always dying in wars. Why should you be reminded of people dying when a church was supposed to be about resurrection? Not that you could have one without the other.

Martha pulled the heavy vacuum cleaner across the red carpet to the right-hand aisle, going carefully over the bumpy cord where the extra sound loop went for the deaf people to hear the preacher man standing at the front. Woman, Martha corrected herself. It had been a woman last week.

She liked the church when it was full of people, but she liked even better to have it all to herself on the day she did the cleaning. At this time of day, with the sun shining as it was now, it was light and warm. The front pew was right in the sun, and Martha sat down in the middle of it. Cliff had shown her a verse in the Bible that said walk in the light, so you might as well sit in it too if you had the chance. In fact, you could lie in it. Martha twisted around and shifted her legs up on the pew and lay, gingerly at first, going slowly into full stretch; she wasn't sure she could keep her balance because the pew wasn't wide, but after a while she began to relax. It was surprisingly comfortable. She put her hands behind her head and looked up. The ceiling needed painting. Cliff would want to have a go at it, but she doubted if Harry would let him. Harry was the maintenance man and ladder climber, and the ceiling was very high.

This is what it would be like lying in this church in your coffin. Coffins were usually parked a little further to the front, but not much. A coffin was just like this: a narrow wooden bed, but with higher sides and satin sheets. Only in a coffin you wouldn't have your hands behind your head, you'd have them straight down, soldierlike at your sides. Maybe that's why they had those soldier plaques, to remind you that you would soon be dead and that you needed to walk and sit and lie in the light while you had the chance.

And then, while Martha was lying there on the pew, but not in a coffin, something fell out of the air and landed with a little thud on her belly. She was so comfortable she didn't move, though she wanted to see what it was. Another thud, this time on her left shin, and then another on her right foot. She took one hand from behind her head and felt on her belly to see what it was. It was a pair of things, round and firm, but giving, with two little stick bits. She lifted them high to see. They were cherries. Two firm round beautiful dark red cherries, plump and ripe, connected by their stems, straight off the tree. She dangled one in her mouth, pulled it from the stalk with her lips, and bit. Sweet thick juice, rich, full-bodied, flooded across her palate. Such cherries! Thud, thud, thud. They were falling faster now, all over her, on her head, on the soft underside of her angled arm, on her face, on her breasts and legs, gathering now in piles between her feet. Cherries falling so thick and fast she could no longer see the ceiling because the air above her was black with cherries. Hills of cherries grew into mountains, rivers of cherries poured through her hair, cherryslides flowed from her body to the floor. Martha tried to think how many cherries there were, how much weight, but she couldn't think, her mind was full of cherry showers, the sweet deep fragrance of them dissolving any attempt at logic, her open mouth catching, teeth bursting them open in little explosions of pleasure.

She lifted both hands and caught them and stuffed them into her mouth. She was hungry for cherries, greedy for cherries, her mouth and chin ran with the red juice. She swung her legs down and sat up and shuffled aside the cherries on the floor to make room for her shoes. The whole church was full of cherries. Every horizontal surface was piled high with them—the seats, the communion table, the piano, the pulpit, the pews.

However would she clean them all up? However would she explain it to Kate and the maintenance committee?

Martha slipped down in her seat, tipped back her head, and started to laugh. She laughed and laughed. She couldn't stop laughing. She laughed until she cried, and she cried so hard that she had to blow her nose. When she looked up from her sodden hankie, she could see the ceiling again, and it still needed painting.

GRIEF was like a disease. Sandra was having a relapse, telling Kate things she had told her before.

"I wasn't there," she said miserably. "He died on his own. Not even a nurse. Nobody should have to die alone."

"I know. It was very difficult."

"They didn't ring me! I don't think they even knew until afterward. They said it was very sudden. I didn't have time to say goodbye."

"I know, it's hard," said Kate, and set aside her serving. "But some things are meant to be. And you'd been saying goodbye ever since the diagnosis, all those walks on the beach, the camping, the theatre outings. All those wonderful special things you did because you had some warning."

Unexpected anger surged through Sandra.

"Stop sanitising it! You know what I mean! I should have been there."

Kate was curiously resistant.

"Jack liked his own company. Perhaps he preferred it that way. Perhaps he wanted to spare you."

Tears prickled. "I'm his *wife!* Well, I *was* his wife. He would have wanted me there. I know he would."

"I called on Jack the day before he died," said Kate. "Remember? Just a quick visit on my way home. He told me he'd had enough. The pain was bad, he wanted to go. And he could see you were tired. He just wanted it over. It was a gift, Sandra, that he didn't linger too long. There are worse things than dying."

"But I wanted to be *there!*"

Kate gave her a long look, stood up, and put her arms around her.

"I know," said Kate. "I know you did."

SANDRA was caught. She had agreed to have Kate's son, Jeremy, to stay while his parents were away for the weekend, but she had forgotten about a colleague's fiftieth birthday party.

Sandra was fond of Jeremy, who was witty and enterprising, and felt badly that she had double-booked.

"Sorry, mate," she said. "But I have to go out tonight. I'll find someone to come and be with you."

Jeremy snorted. "I can look after myself."

"I'm sure you can. But I feel responsible."

"Mum and Dad leave me home alone all the time."

"Oh, right. For weeks at a time, no doubt. So you can throw wild parties and still have time to clean up."

Jeremy grinned. "Once they came home and I had the whole class there. We were all drunk."

Sandra cuffed him softly.

"You are so full of it, my lad. Your mother won't even let you walk to school by yourself."

Jeremy sighed. "I know. Tell her to ease up, Sander. I'm nearly a teenager." Kate had always been a little overprotective.

"OK. I'll see what I can do. But no promises."

Jeremy danced around the table singing, shaking his finger at his imaginary mother.

"Naughty Kate, naughty Kate! Won't let Jezza stay up late!"

Sandra browsed through the Yellow Pages. She had often envied Kate and Tony their parenthood, but as Jeremy got bigger and louder she wondered if she would have had the stamina.

She had never had to find a babysitter in her life. How did you know if one was reputable? She rang the friends she and Kate had in common whom she felt able to ask, but they were busy doing other things. If she didn't find someone soon, she'd have to miss the party.

Sandra called Kate's mobile. Kate couldn't think of anyone else who would be free at such short notice.

"Martha? What about Martha?" Sandra said. "She doesn't have too many commitments."

"I wouldn't make assumptions," said Kate. "But yes, ask Martha by all means. Jeremy doesn't know her very well, but he'll cope." She had a few words with Jeremy and then hung up.

Sandra dialled Martha's number.

"Martha, I know this is out of the blue and very short notice, but I'm looking after Kate's son for the weekend. I forgot I have to go out for a couple of hours. Would you be able to help me out? I'm happy to pay you, of course."

"How old is he?"

"Twelve. Old enough to look after himself, really, but I don't want to leave him on his own. He won't be any trouble. He's been glued to the Internet all day. All you'll have to do is prise him off at bedtime. I checked with Kate. She's fine about it."

"Should be all right. He's not a baby. At least he can wipe his own bum."

"Well, yes, I'm sure he can." Was Martha joking or was it a serious consideration? Sandra wasn't sure. "Thanks, Martha. I'll pick you up at six."

MARTHA and Jeremy eyed each other up and down. The boy from next door who had come to keep Jeremy company gave him an exaggerated wink. Sandra sent him home and kissed Jeremy on top of his head.

"Won't be long, mate. You can use the computer till ten, then you have to go to bed. Behave yourself. Thanks, Martha." She was off.

Martha could not settle in Sandra's house. It was all hard surfaces and straight lines, and so uncluttered she could hardly breathe. Even the carnations on the dining room table had an angularity to them. She stopped reading the magazine and went to stand by Jeremy, who was surfing the Net on Sandra's computer.

When Martha came to look, Jeremy, accustomed to adult ignorance, showed off, leaning back in his chair with the mouse on the desk in front of him at arm's length. Click click click. Martha couldn't keep up, but she knew that this was a way to find information, any information, all information, anywhere in the world. She pulled up a chair.

"Slow down a bit, Jerry. Show me how it works."

Jeremy groaned. "I'm looking for cheat files for my new game."

"You can do that any time."

Jeremy groaned again. Martha ignored him. He zoomed the mouse around the pad a few more times.

"What do you want to know?"

"I want to find out about knitting. Get some patterns and that. Find other knitters."

Jeremy rolled his eyes up so only the whites showed and turned his face toward her.

"They don't have that stuff on computers."

"Yes, they do. I know they do. Come on, Jerry."

"What will you pay me?"

Martha did not flinch.

"I'll give you ten bucks to show me how it works. For one whole hour. But you're working for me. You got that? Because I'm paying you. I'm paying you to teach me properly. So just start at the beginning, and go slow."

"Fifteen."

Martha pulled up closer. Jeremy felt Martha's heat radiating onto his skinny arms. She was burning like the sun.

"Ten, ya lazy little bludger." To Jeremy's surprise she took a ten-dollar bill from her bra and waved it under his nose. "All you have to do is sit on your bum and talk. It's not like you're mowing the lawn or anything. If you don't want it, I'll ask that neighbour kid who was here before, Anthony, whatever his name is."

Jeremy caved in.

"OK." He looked at his watch. "But at eight-thirty-four exactly you have to stop and leave me alone." He knew better than Martha that it would be hard to stop. He took a deep breath and spoke slowly and deliberately, as though quoting from a book.

"This is called the desktop. And all these little icons are like the drawers in your desk. And in the drawers are folders, and in each folder are programs or documents." Martha was surprised at how clearly and logically he explained it. Jeremy in turn was surprised that Martha seemed to understand, though she had some trouble with the mouse. Martha had gone to the free lessons at the library the week before, but she didn't tell Jeremy that.

After Martha had mastered search engines, down-loaded some feather-stitch patterns that took her fancy, and looked at instructions for argyle socks, he showed her a chat room.

"You can call yourself anything you like. And never give your real address. Else they'll come and get you one day, and rip off your stuff."

"What should I call myself?"

"I dunno."

"Madmartha," keyed Jeremy, and looked around at Martha to see a fleeting dismay. Then she grinned.

There were three people in the chat room: Sockit-tome from Canada, Wendy in the UK, and Fiddlesticks in New Zealand. Martha was pink with excitement.

"Get Madmartha to write this," said Martha. "How do you get a knitted horse to stand up by itself?"

"No one will know that."

"Do it."

Jeremy was bored, but he did as he was told. He was watching the clock at the corner of the screen. A reply appeared from Fiddlesticks in New Zealand. Martha clapped her hands and started to read aloud.

"'How big is it?' Tell her it's as big as—hey, what happened?"

The screen flickered and the desktop reappeared. Jeremy had closed the browser. Martha stared at the screen.

"Time's up. It's eight-thirty-five. I gave you one minute for free. You owe me ten bucks."

Martha handed over the ten dollars with a peculiar look on her face. She stood up and put her chair back under the table. Then she took his face in her hand, turning it so she could look him in the eye. She squeezed his cheeks in a pincer grip so that his mouth puffed into fish lips.

"Do you know what, Jeremy Big Fat Joker? That is the first time I have ever talked to someone in another country. And I wanted the answer to that question because I've been having trouble with my horse. You can play computers any bloody old time you like, here or at your place, and I hardly ever get a chance. You are a giant green snot." She reached out and pressed the big button on the computer. She wasn't sure what it did, but it looked like a good bet. The screen died. She looked at her watch.

"Well, look at that. Eight-thirty-six, and I'm thinking you need an early night. There are some magazines under that coffee table if you want to read for a while. But no more computer, that's for sure."

She thought he would protest, but he didn't. He looked shamefaced. Good. Let him learn to respect his elders. When he meekly shut the bedroom door she turned on the computer again. Eventually she remembered how to manage searches. She couldn't find the chat room again, but she had fun frolicking through knitting sites.

OCTOBER

IT WAS A long way to Wollongong, on the east coast. Sandra had traveled a day early to avoid the six a.m. flight, but it took most of the day to get there all the same. The grumpy cab driver, then that unexplained delay at the airport. Sandra scored a window seat—she liked to be tucked out of the way of food carts and passengers—and the seat next to her was empty. But the aisle seat was occupied by a young businessman with a laptop who, though he looked like an experienced traveller, was distinctly agitated during takeoff and landing. His nervousness was contagious. She could hear a loose buzzing noise behind the window next to her head. Was the plane about to disintegrate? Then the wait in Sydney for the transit bus, the long traffic-slowed ride to Wollongong. In the stuffy university flat, her presence seemed no more significant than a beetle's. She threw her bags on the bed and opened the windows to let in the breeze. Her first conference since Jack's death. No one to call and say she had safely arrived.

She wasn't giving a paper. "Just going for the ride," she had said to Kate. "It's textiles based—'Material Girls: Fabric and Feminism'—though I'm more interested in the history." She would not confess, even to Kate, that of all the events in the four-day program it was the day-long knitting workshop that had captured her attention. Although she had never been good with her hands, she wanted to have another try. Some inner self was dissatisfied. Perhaps handwork of some kind would answer it.

Sandra had found that she was losing interest in words. She could barely articulate to herself the sense of widening gap, a crevasse between what she wanted to say and what she could express, the yearning for which she had no language. Words had always been enough in the past; words, she had frequently said to her students, could do anything, take you anywhere. In the beginning was the Word. Words had no limitations; with words you could tunnel through mountains of theory, construct arguments like suspension bridges. She would recount her joy as a six-year-old discovering that the words she spoke were only one language, that there were hundreds of other ways of saying the same thing, often with more nuance.

Language and literacy, she said to her students, were a powerful combination, giving access to all the information in the world. Words were energy, dynamic: they moved around, through, over, under. At this juncture she would turn and write on the board "over my head", "think things through", "understated", and invite further contributions from the class.

Sandra was a word gobbler. In her childhood she had read compulsively, everything from cereal boxes to her father's law books. All her life she had stuffed words into herself—books, articles, conferences, workshops. At times her brain ached with distension. Her whole body was pinched and pinned by words: the backache from being too long at the computer, the pain of hands pounding at the keyboard. She had been making and unmaking words her whole life, floods of words that threatened to overflow the poor channels she made for them and spill across the flat Australian plains of her life, swirling with mud and debris. There were times she wished she could stop the flood, wished there were another way to say things.

She dragged a heavy, student-proof steel chair out onto the balcony, ordered food from a take-away, and sat in the evening with an orange juice poured from "breakfast provided".

But the fact was that words had their limitations. There were some things in life, feelings, experiences, for which there were no names. There were no words for the joy she had shared with Jack, and no words for losing him. No words for this mindlessness, this absence.

Jack had enjoyed words, too, but Jack was different. If

Sandra was awash with words, Jack had nurtured his. His words were short and stumpy, firmly rooted. Not often bitter. And Jack was funny; he had thrown his sense of the absurd like a life preserver to Sandra when her rivers of words threatened to drown her. Jack's words, slow grown, nourished by deep silences, were rarely wasted. His first draft was almost always his last. Sandra had to sift and strain, edit the flotsam and jetsam that poured willy-nilly with the intended meaning. Revise, revise, she told her students, and followed her own advice. But she could find no words at all for this inner space, the vacuum inside the hard, bright glass of her existence. She hadn't written anything since the onset of Jack's illness, relying instead on old habits, old secondhand words for her lectures. Her teaching had become dishonest.

She had not slept well the night before her departure for Wollongong and went to bed early. The mattress was bumpy, her hip hurt. And then something started stinging her face. She slapped at it a few times before turning the light on to find that her sheet and pillow were covered with tiny black moving spots. They were too small to distinguish legs. Where had they come from? Had she brushed a web on the balcony, dislodged a nest of baby spiders?

She threw back the sheet and looked for telltale signs, but there were none. She squashed as many as she could see, leaving smears like pen marks on the white sheets, some of them dark red with her blood. She tried again to sleep.

It was impossible. They were in her hair now, crawling on her scalp, and there seemed to be more than before. It was a nightmare; she was tired, half crazy with lack of sleep. Her face burned and itched. At three in the morning she showered and washed her hair, put on fresh clothes, and remade the bed. For half an hour she had relative peace, then the crawling started again. Finally, as it grew light, the sensations diminished. She slept for an hour but awoke scratching her face. The black spots had disappeared, but her face was red and swollen with evidence. She showered again, ate a Granny Smith from the fridge, and plastered on her makeup thickly to cover the welts.

She rang the conference organiser to ask for a change of bedding and flyspray. The organiser apologised profusely. Sandra was too tired to be angry.

"Is there a chemist on campus?"

"No. But there's one within walking distance."

There wasn't time to go to the chemist. Self-conscious about her inflamed face, fuzzy from lack of sleep, Sandra made her way through the maze of buildings to the knitting workshop.

The facilitator was Clare Young, a free-form knitter. The room was festooned with Clare's garish art—the prime minister as a merman among knitted shells and starfish, caught in a large knitted web that he himself was making. A knitted businesswoman wearing a lacy knitted apron over her suit. A grossly misshapen headless female torso with a crocheted hat on the neck stump. Sandra looked around in dismay. She should never have come.

Participants were emptying their bags of wool scraps onto the table while Clare pinned up flower images: lilies, roses, daisies, their grace and purity of form at odds with Clare's ugly derivations. Sandra had forgotten to bring wool scraps and needles. She went to the corner and made herself a strong coffee thick with sugar. Wake up, wake up, don't panic. It will be all right.

"Choose a flower," shouted Clare enthusiastically. "A meaningful image. One you care about. Then think about its counterpart, the worm, the slug, the aphid." She turned the prime minister's head around to demonstrate a hollow cross section in the rear of the skull. "See? White ants."

Sandra found herself rebelling. She didn't want to concentrate on her dark side, on any layering of complexity. Life was difficult enough. She would lodge her own protest, go for simplicity, make something that was just as it appeared. She stared at a close-up of pale yellow Peace roses tinged with pink.

"The technique is simple, just good old-fashioned knitting stitches." Clare distributed pattern diagrams. "You start with a petal or a leaf and go on from there. Draw a shape if you like, and then knit to the shape. Learn to do these small things, and you can adjust the technique to larger forms."

Clare led them through the steps, showed them how to splice their yarn for gradual shades, how to shape the petals by casting on and casting off, how to pick up along knitted edges, increase and decrease. First they made leaves, then started on their flowers. The man next to Sandra was making a Sturt's desert pea with shiny black metallic thread, exaggerating the scarlet petals so that they drooped from his lap to the floor. Inside the flower was a small white grub. He was a deft worker, his plump hands quick and sure. He called it "Invasion".

Sandra worried away at her rose, listening to the others talking — artists, teachers, curators, academics — obviously part of a well-established network. No one was taking the workshop seriously, which was both comforting and disappointing. Sandra had hoped for more, something beyond the reach of words. With so little sleep, she felt surprisingly alert now, thanks to coffee. The work wasn't as easy as it looked, though she was pleased with the first petal and better pleased with the next, merging cream through shades of pink. Working on a Peace rose, at the edge of peace: the metaphor amused her. But when she tried to make the calyx, the petals were loose; the flower drooped on its stem as though it needed water.

The workshop broke for lunch. Out in the foyer were tables laden with a variety of breads made into open sandwiches, with apples, tangelos, and bottles of spring water. The vegetarian rolls disappeared; the ham-and-mustards were left to dry on the platter.

After lunch Sandra tried experimenting, using a feather stitch as the basis for a flower petal, but her heart wasn't in it, and besides, it was just too difficult. Fatigue had set in; knitted flowers suddenly seemed ridiculous. She picked up her floppy attempt at a rose and went back to the flat for a nap. When she fished in her handbag for the key, she found that the rose had disappeared. No peace for me, she thought wryly, and felt the sudden prick of tears.

After the nap she felt better. The insects had disappeared. Another woman, also from Adelaide, a journalist, came to share the flat. A big woman, she was energetic and cheerful, and soon had Sandra laughing in spite of herself. She knew a great deal about knitting and, to Sandra's surprise, knew also of Martha. She told Sandra about another knitter, Ruby Brilliant, and how moved she had been by the pieces styled on priests' chasubles.

"Crucifixion, Passion, Ascension," she said. "Knitted. *Knitted!*" Sandra was wary—that was all she needed, a large, loud born-again—but the topic stopped there. And it was good to have someone to walk with, to share a meal in the evenings, to discuss the day's events, to hear her confession that although she was a member of the Spinners and Weavers Guild, she too was hopeless with her hands. They discussed the keynote speaker, Jonty Stewart, at some length, and the gap between practice and theory.

Sandra began to relax and to enjoy the conference. There was no need to disclose personal details; Jack didn't get a mention. Life was easy if you kept it superficial.

BACK at home, Sandra had another look at the article on Greek artifacts. Spinning, weaving, knitting, all part of the long tradition of women's work, skills that had survived even the efficiency of the industrial revolution. Why did people still do it? The techniques hadn't changed, even if needles were now made of plastic and colours were commercial dyes.

Martha had a spinning wheel and an old-fashioned spindle as well, Sandra had seen, a relic from the late seventies, no doubt, when spinning and weaving had flourished. Did Martha still use the spindle? It looked handy enough there in the corner, tossed on top of a basket of dark fleece.

The spindle had been simple chipboard—no elaborate carving here, like the god's eye on the Greek stone spindles. Judging by the photographs with the article, little had changed in a couple of thousand years. Perhaps the ancients had had wooden spindles, too, but they had rotted away.

Sandra had never learned to spin and, though she had learned the basics of knitting, was sure she'd never be a real knitter. It was too slow. At the workshop she had been clumsy and awkward with the needles: the stitches were too tight or too loose, and in the beginning they had increased or decreased of their own accord. She was better at words; she could make even the most convoluted theory accessible to her students if she stayed patient enough. In spite of their limitations, words were more malleable, more cooperative; they strung themselves evenly along the straight line of argument, and it was easy to see the holes and puckers, to straighten out the bumps.

Ancient language, ancient skills. Stories and spinning. It would be fun to have some kind of exhibition. Clothing, perhaps. Everyday textiles, everyday words, fragments of oral history. Sandra started a tentative list.

Text and textiles? No. Boring.

Words and wool? Wool and words? Too corny.

Fact and fabric. Who believed in facts?

Textuality. Maybe. No, *Textu(r)ality.* That was it, text, texture, textile, context, all there or implied. A title to make you think. She wrote down the word in capitals and drew a line under it.

Years ago she had written a paper on women's domestic work, focusing on textiles. Most of her interviewees had been older women, whose ordered lives she envied. Yes, they sewed, and knitted, and crocheted—or used to once. So what? Everybody did. Now they were painting and travelling or getting the education they had missed. "Back in the old days," one of them said, "running a house took all your time. Food and clothes and kids—that was our job. The men brought home the bacon. That was their job. I think you modern girls have it tough, doing everything." Well-defined roles, defined times for work, defined times to relax peacefully in the evening and knit by the radio or TV. Sandra remembered her own mother's life with nostalgia, and despised herself for it. No pay. Remember that.

Not all women had been like that, of course. She had aunts who had worked for a paycheque, politically argumentative women who could knit and read interesting books simultaneously. In Sandra's youth it was mainly single women who worked. Later, working herself, she saw colleagues caught in the tug of war between work and family, saw the puffiness around their eyes, the guilty cost of the juggling act. And though she had longed for children once, perhaps it was better this way; if she was allowed only one of the two, at least she had travelled freely and enjoyed her career. Though now that Jack was gone, she worried sometimes about growing old alone.

She had stashed hard copy of her favourite interview pieces in a folder somewhere. Plenty of material there for mining. But it was more than the textiles, it was the way the women had talked about them, and the breadth of subject matter, that had fascinated her. Social history knitted in snippets of everyday language: a trouser fly deliberately sewn up, a child's jumper sleeve picked up on the needles for extension, the seat of a pair of jeans made into a baby bag, wartime socks knitted during church. Conversation, dialogue, all the same substance, but fragmentary, just like those ancient scraps of linen. Yes, she could see it now, narrative fragments in various forms, mounted between the garments, text and texture creating their own dynamic. She smiled broadly and caught herself at it.

And Martha, what a find! Martha, still working in the direct line of the ancient traditions, spinning and knitting. Women's work, indeed, but the inventiveness! That crazy horse! And the graciousness of her gift, the silver shawl. Sandra's mind was twirling in the dance now. Implications of empowering . . . Ariadne's thread, kill the Minotaur and find your way out of the suffocating darkness, the way back home.

The exhibition would need parameters of some sort. The last hundred years, perhaps, with hints of the past and future. Knitted garments. Of course! Hand-knitted, to keep the field narrow. And there was Martha, just waiting to happen. Unlike weaving, knitting was a relatively recent development, only about a thousand years old, but it was a tangible link, a strong branch of the great historical flow that was still evident in modern households. And it provided a basic framework.

Textu(r)ality: an exhibition of knitted garments in all their variety, joined and juxtaposed with text, with constructions of text. She had been waiting for something like this ever since Jack died. Teaching was demanding, but there was a sameness to it; she had learned to go with the ebb and flow of the intense periods, to ride them out. But teaching wasn't enough any more; she was restless, needed a change, a new project away from teaching. A little exhibition in a hall somewhere, away from work—it didn't have to be too serious. Her career wasn't hanging on it, though maybe her sanity was.

She must send an e-mail to her flat-mate from Wollongong and go to see Martha. Martha—what an opportunity for Martha to showcase her work! Martha would never look back.

It was a hot spring day that smelled of summer. Martha and Sandra were lying on the green grass by Sandra's swimming pool. Sandra had locked the gate and was lying face down and topless in the full sun, thinking about the proposed exhibition. She had invited Martha over for lunch and a swim, on the pretext of returning the patterns she had borrowed when they had lunch with Kate. She wanted to discuss the exhibition but had not found a way to articulate it without sounding as though she was simply using Martha. Members of the Spinners and Weavers Guild would provide some garments, but so far they didn't seem to have everything she wanted. While there were more old knits available than she had expected, there wasn't the range she wanted, especially from the first twenty years of the 1900s. Even if they had survived the moths, they'd been recycled during the Second World War, unravelled and reknitted, the scrappy pieces sewn into quilts as a middle layer for warmth.

She hadn't mentioned the project to Martha yet. There just hadn't been the right opportunity, even though they had shared coffee more than once. Martha, she was learning, could be unpredictable, and Sandra wanted to choose her moment. Working together would change their relationship, and she wanted to start well.

Martha was lying face up with her head in the shade of the Queensland box tree.

"This darn tree's raining leaves on me," said Martha, flicking one from her face.

"It always does that in the first heat. Makes a mess in the swimming pool. Jack was always fishing them out. Now I leave them for the pool man." Sandra was talking into the grass. Martha turned her head sideways to hear better, and saw that Sandra was lying like a broken bird, all ribs and elbows and messy feathers. On Martha's other side the pool glinted clear blue.

"Cliff would like it here," said Martha.

Sandra settled deeper into the towel but half turned her face so Martha could see one eye, half a nose, and half a mouth behind stems of green grass.

"Yes, but if Cliff was here, I couldn't take my top off. He'd be too embarrassed."

"You mean you would be," said Martha.

"No, he would be. *I* wouldn't care."

"Yes, you would," said Martha stoutly. "I bet you wouldn't just sit there and take it off, like you did a minute ago."

Martha was beginning to grate. Sandra sat up, suddenly self-conscious. "Martha, you shouldn't pretend you can get inside my head."

"Shouldn't say 'shouldn't' " said Martha. "You're supposed to say, 'I don't like it when you say things like that.' "

"Who said?"

"The leader of a group I was in once."

Sandra rolled her eyes, started to work out a convoluted reply, and then gave up.

"It's Sunday, Martha. Give me a break. It's a day to relax, not have a group therapy session." She saw that the shadow of the pool safety fence had crept over Martha's solid body in her floral bathing suit, covering her in a series of parallel lines.

"Look, Martha," Sandra said to change the subject. "You're in a cage."

Martha got up on her elbows to see what Sandra meant. She moved one arm slowly and watched the shadows ripple across her skin.

"A shadow cage," said Martha. "I can't break the bars, but at least I can get out." She straightened her arms above her head and rolled over heavily a couple of times till she bumped into Sandra.

"Oops."

Sandra was reaching for her shirt. Martha had no idea of personal space.

"I'm getting dressed. Do you want another swim before I take you home?" She heard her own voice, disguising coercion as generosity. The exhibition business would have to wait.

NOVEMBER

IT WAS HOT, the third day straight over thirty-five Celsius, and it was going to get worse. Summer had not even begun. Summer and the beach. Summer and the beach and all those memories she and Jack had made together.

It had been hot that other day, too, three or four years ago, when the air conditioning in the car had broken down, and suddenly Jack had swung down an unfamiliar side road. They parked at the top of a cliff among the other empty cars and ran down the steps. Dotted around the beach were flaccid white lumps turning various shades of pink.

"What is this place?"

"Maslins Beach. Legal nudity."

Jack dumped their towels near a bumpy old couple in their sixties and started to strip.

"Race you in," he said.

Sandra, caught up in Jack's enthusiasm, was suddenly snagged.

She stared around her, felt her body shrink into itself. "Can't do it," she said. "Too many people."

"Too many people with their clothes off?" asked Jack.

"No. Too many people watching."

"Oh, come on," said Jack. "As if they'd care. Besides, you're nearly fifty, my darling. Time to face the facts. Who's going to look at us with our saggy bits? They come here to gawk at the young ones." He grinned at her over his hairy chest. They were both pasty white.

She turned her back on the old couple and draped a towel around herself before stepping out of her clothes, then followed him gingerly across the soft white sand to the hard flat surface near the water. She dropped her towel reluctantly, just out of reach of the waves, and followed him in.

Jack was ahead of her under the green water. The sea was almost flat, but Sandra gasped with shock as the swell of water rose against her chest.

She stopped watching Jack. Bending her knees, she looked at her hands floating eerily under the water, then gradually lowered herself until she was wet up to her neck. Jack was swimming out to sea in an easy freestyle. She peered around, looking for prying eyes. Gradually she relaxed and let the water take her. She flipped to her back, swaying on the surface like a clump of floating seaweed. She must look like a series of floating islands. It was good out here.

Suddenly something grasped at her ankle. She cried out in alarm, but it was only Jack, upending her, pulling her off balance so that she was forced to tread water. He twisted around to catch her from behind, cupping her breasts in his hands and putting his salty mouth against her ear.

"Mm, what's this I've caught in my net? A real live mermaid. Come and live with me, mermaid, and I'll show you how we landlubbers enjoy ourselves." She elbowed him in the chest and kicked away backward.

"I'm no mermaid! No man is worth cut feet!" She was surprised at her own strength, how the distance between them increased more rapidly than she expected.

"Hey, come back!" Jack shouted. She started back towards him but couldn't make any headway.

"You're in a rip! Swim sideways." He waved his hand parallel to the shore.

Panic surged up like vomit.

Mustn't panic, she said to herself. Get a grip. Swim. She looked toward the beach to get her bearings, but it made things worse; it was much farther than she had thought.

"Jack! Help!" Her swimming was feeble.

Jack had seen that to catch her he too had to enter the rip. He came close but not close enough to touch.

"Sandy! Look at me!" She was gulping fiercely. "Calm down. We can get out. It's not that far. Don't grab me, or we'll both go under. Turn over on your back. Float."

She wouldn't turn over. She was scared to lose sight of him.

"When you're on your back, I'll grab your hair. You paddle your hands and kick. Go on! Trust me!"

She still hesitated.

"Do it!"

She hadn't heard that tone for many years. It frightened her into action. She felt his hand wrap firmly in her hair, the strong kick of his leg at her side. She resisted the overwhelming urge to grab at him and began to kick.

He lifted her head out of the water so she could hear him. "Good. Keep it up. Straighten your legs, you'll kick better."

It was slow work getting back.

All of a sudden he let go of her. She flipped toward him in panic, then felt her foot touch bottom. The water was still up to her neck.

"Come on, we can walk now. Here." He reached back for her hand.

She couldn't speak.

"Ah, little mermaid, I see you've got legs after all."

"My tail doesn't work."

"I wouldn't be so sure of that."

Back by their clothes the elderly couple smiled at them.

"Got to watch that rip, love," the woman said. "Lucky

you've got him. You're not the first, either. They could do with some lifeguards round here." She went on creaming her pendulous breasts.

That night, showered and fed, as they read comfortably in bed, Jack turned to look at her.

"Are you OK?"

Tears welled up.

"I was terrified."

"You were great. Lots of people can't fight the panic. Even though they know how to swim, they drown anyway."

"I would have if you weren't there."

She wanted to thank him, but part of her held back, feeling raw and exposed.

"What's the matter?"

"Nothing."

He had turned fully toward her.

"Yes, there is. What is it?"

It took a few seconds to steady her voice. "I nearly drowned."

"Not even close. You were still thinking, still working to save yourself."

But she had almost drowned, she knew. When she kissed him later, she could taste her own desperation.

SANDRA had finally broached the subject of the exhibition. She would need Martha to knit twenty or so garments from old patterns, from before 1950. She wanted variety—she had already ferreted out patterns for garments with strange names: a fishing guernsey, lady's sleeping suit, sailor's steering glove, and child's bootiken. Martha was fascinated by the patterns but did not take to the opportunity of showcasing her work.

"I'm just a home knitter, that's all."

"No you're not, Martha. You're brilliant. You must know that. And this will be simple stuff for you. You're capable of work way beyond this. You're a real artist, the way you challenge ideas, experiment with fibre and colour. Look at those wall hangings or that horse sculpture—that's not home knitting, that's art."

"It is home knitting," said Martha stubbornly. "I do it at home. I do it for fun, or for people I care about. I'm just mucking around, that's all, having fun. You make it sound important, like a kind of work. Well, it is work, but it's happy work, work that I like, that I do when I'm in the mood. But if I have to do it, I might not like it any more. I won't be able to choose it. I don't like deadlines. I crack up when I get too busy, with too much stuff in my head. My work needs to be playing."

Sandra thought she understood; she knew how it felt when boundaries between work and play dissolved, when payment was less important than satisfaction. How to win Martha over?

"Most people get up in the morning and choose to go to work. So do you, if you think about it. And you'd be able to earn some money. I hope to get a grant."

"I don't need money. I get on fine."

"Well, the grant wouldn't be much. We need to hire the space, print the catalogues, pay for the mounting. But you could sell your garments for good prices, a few hundred dollars each. And no commission, either—I think we could arrange that. Some of the clothes will be old—that's if we can find them—clothes from every decade in the last century. But there's some particular items I want, like knitted bloomers, and those old bathing suits men used to wear, so there'll be gaps to fill. I want to concentrate on knitted garments, and woollen ones at that, because it's the fact that it's knitting that defines the parameters. I'm still not sure what's readily available. The trouble with wool is that during the Depression and the war, every spare bit was recycled for warmth. And of course moths get into it. But sometimes families keep things stuffed away in mothballs for years and years, so we'll just have to see what we get . . . And it's part of our heritage—Australia and sheep and all that. Would you do some hand-spinning?"

"What, instead?"

"No, as well as."

"You don't need me for that. Go to the Spinners and Weavers Guild. There are plenty of knitters and spinners in Adelaide. I'll give you the addresses."

"But I want *you*. We can work together."

"Not spinning. I can do it, but I don't want to. There's something about that wheel going round and round in circles that drives me crazy."

"Oh, all right, I guess I can find a spinner. But you're the knitter. This is the chance of a lifetime, Martha! This could turn into full-time work for you! An exhibition like this is advertised in magazines and newspapers; the arts people will come flocking. They'll all be wanting your clothes, you'll see. You might even get an order from the prime minister or some famous actor."

"I've knitted jumpers for actors before. And the prime minister can jump in the lake. I don't approve of him."

Sandra tried a different tack.

"Martha, this is something I've wanted to do for a long time. Look, I want to put on a show that combines words and textiles. It was you who inspired me. Women have been doing this for centuries, making things. And in the act of making things, just by living their daily lives, they also make history. That's the story I want to tell, the story of the making. That's *my* making, if you like. I've had this idea for a long time, but women have made so many things that I didn't know how to narrow the field.

"Then you came along with your knitting. It was you, don't you see? Knitting is clothing made in spare moments, or round the fire, whenever women gathered together. People like you are keeping this skill alive. It's something to celebrate—clothes made in love and service, something women have always done."

"Men used to knit, before women."

Martha just didn't get it. Sandra kept on talking, pouring words into the space between them, which yawned even wider as she spoke.

"It's hard to explain. But the word stuff is my side and I'd like you to do the knitting. Two people, making things, me collecting words and putting pieces of text together, and you collecting wool and knitting garments."

"You're making a big fuss about nothing, Sandra. Knitting's just for keeping warm. And for a bit of fun. The horse is only fun. It doesn't have to mean anything."

Sandra wanted to shake Martha till her teeth rattled, but she threw herself back in the chair instead, in a comic display of despair. Martha looked at her. Sandra reminded her of a floppy rag doll that was starting to fall apart. In fact, Sandra would fall apart if Martha didn't help her. Martha could see Sandra needed help, but it might be costly . . . Sandra had no idea what it might cost Martha.

"It's really important to you, isn't it, all this business?"

"Yes."

When it came to the crunch, Martha believed that others' interests should be put ahead of one's own.

"OK. I'll do it. But not for all that arty-farty stuff. I'll do it because you're my friend. Only—"

"Only what?"

Martha shrugged, and then smiled. "Never mind. You're my friend."

THE weeks before the first anniversary of Jack's death plodded by. On the day itself, October 29, Sandra worked flat out so she didn't have to think. The following week, in the first flush of having survived a whole year alone, Sandra found herself oddly cheerful, buoyant with anticipation. It was a long time since she had felt like this.

Kate and Tony and Martha and Sandra were going to Port MacDonnell for the first week in December. In the old days it had been Jack and Sandra, Tony and Kate. When Kate first introduced Sandra to Tony, all those years ago, Sandra was alarmed on Kate's behalf. She couldn't imagine anyone being happy with this loud, brash, opinionated businessman. But over the years she had discovered a different side to Tony—his loyalty, an unexpected generosity, a deep kindness behind the noisy exterior. After Jack died he had helped her, night after night, sorting through paperwork, until she understood it properly.

Originally the week away was to celebrate Tony's selling one business and buying another. It was the ideal time for a break, and Jeremy would be on holiday in Perth with relatives. Kate and Tony's plan coincided with Sandra's own time off. While she had not been specifically invited to go with them, it never occurred to Sandra that she might not be welcome. She and Jack had shared many such occasions with Kate and Tony, and she invited Martha without checking with them.

It would be a good week. Tony would hibernate like a

big brown bear in his crime novels and leave the three women free to plan the exhibition. It was play rather than work, a *holiday*, Sandra told Martha, though the idea of a holiday seemed foreign to Martha's thinking.

During November, Sandra and Martha spent three weekends scouring op shops for old knitting patterns, with more success than Sandra had anticipated. In the shop that looked the least promising she found a small blue leather case, one lock sprung open and refusing to close, full of knitting books and patterns. An auctioneer's job lot, an estate sale probably, maybe a dollar at the end of a long day. The woman behind the counter must have seen Sandra's look of joy. She charged her twenty dollars. Martha watched, bemused, and said later that she should have bargained, but Sandra was pleased with her purchase and considered it cheap.

A few days before leaving, Sandra looked through her personal collection of retro woollen garments. Why she had developed this particular passion she was not sure — it had something to do with the texture, the cosy warmth, the tradition of women providing for their families, the smell of mothballs. Her mother knitting was one of Sandra's enduring memories, and Sandra still had a couple of items her mother had made in the 1940s. The other garments were all postwar. She hoped that by going through the patterns with Kate and Martha, they could choose some items for Martha to make and fill in the gaps.

In spite of their differences Sandra had grown fond of Martha. She was funny, and Sandra found her company strangely refreshing. You were never sure what she would say or do next; she was an enigma, creative and capable but a bit strange. Socially awkward was perhaps a better term, though not quite that either. She got on with people well enough. She was just different.

Sandra was sure of Martha's need for a holiday, even if Martha wasn't. Preparing for the exhibition would require a long, concentrated effort. Besides, Martha would benefit from some company: her social life seemed rather limited, though Kate told Sandra that Martha had become a regular at church, or at least at coffee afterward. Unlike the previous cleaner, she didn't get upset about mess.

"Don't worry about the floor," Kate had overheard Martha saying to Cliff. "If you don't drop crumbs I won't have a job."

But for some reason she seemed almost resistant to the idea of the holiday.

"Are you sure I'm invited?" Martha asked Sandra.

"Yes. I'm inviting you right now."

"It's a bit close to Christmas. I've got things to do."

"You'll have plenty of time, Martha. It's only one week. And you can bring your knitting."

"What if I don't come?" asked Martha. "Would you ask some other odd-bod, like Cliff?"

Cliff! Why was she so solicitous about Cliff? Sandra tried to be patient.

"I'd be disappointed. Besides, it's too late to ask Cliff. And it's really Kate and Tony's weekend."

Martha raised her eyebrows.

"Are some people better value than others?"

"I don't want Cliff," said Sandra firmly. "I asked you. I want you to come. If you don't come, I won't go."

"Couldn't Cliff come too? Poor old bugger could do with a change."

The hot flush was climbing into Sandra's scalp.

"There's no room," she said. "We only want to take one car. And it would be presuming on the others. We'll ask Cliff another time." Martha was looking at her steadily.

"Well," said Sandra. "Are you coming or not?"

"Why me, though?" said Martha.

Sandra laughed, trying to make it light,

"Your expertise. And your company. And so we can do some planning for the exhibition." Her answer was quick and airy, but she felt cross. Kate and Tony could have their religion—loving your neighbour was too bloody difficult.

But she knew her persistence wasn't really about Martha. It was more about filling the gaping hole of Jack's absence.

December

They arrived at the beach house right on sunset.

"Guess I'll be the hunter, then," said Tony, and went off to find the key, hidden in a screw-top jar under a geranium. He came back waving it triumphantly. They trooped in like schoolchildren inspecting a new classroom.

The house was more modern than they had expected.

"Wow," said Martha.

"Dishwasher," said Kate.

"No, I mean the chairs," said Martha, pointing to the white, billowy living room furniture. "Look at that. Like clouds." She sat in one sideways and dangled her feet over the armrest. There was no TV. They would have to entertain themselves.

They brought in food and made beds. Martha, suddenly talkative, announced that she'd sleep in the same room as Sandra so they could have "nice little chats," but Sandra said she snored and didn't want to keep anyone awake, and besides, there was plenty of room.

"I don't mind," said Martha.

"Well, I do. I'd stay awake all night trying not to snore."

"What's this box?" asked Tony, lugging in a large lid-ded plastic box. "This is over your luggage limit, Sandra! And Martha, all those bags! Anyone would think we're here for a year."

"Knitting patterns, nineteen hundred to two thou-sand," said Sandra in an announcer's voice.

"I need those bags," said Martha.

"This is a holiday," protested Tony.

"What have you got in these things, Martha?" He grunted as he pulled her luggage from the car.

"Knitting. Stuff I might need. And this little bag"— she indicated a small pillowcase—"is the knitting I was doing in the car." Sandra, sitting next to Martha in the back seat, had seen it and asked what it was. "Part of a dress," Martha had said. The yarn was fine and white, like baby wool. Sandra hadn't been able to make sense of the shape.

"Who's it for?" she had asked.

Martha acted as though she hadn't heard. After a long silence during which she sat prim and tight, she relented enough to smooth it out and show Sandra the pattern. It looked like a dense pattern of whorls.

"The pattern's called roseheart."

Sandra saw it then. A pattern of rosebuds, each centered in a lace diamond. "Lovely," she said. "But what shape is it? I can't see how this is part of anything."

"It's part of the top," said Martha, and snapped shut again for the next hundred kilometres.

SATURDAY morning they ate a long, leisurely breakfast, then draped themselves about the house to read. They had a whole week ahead of them, there was no urgency. Even the flat sea, visible through the broad front windows, lazed quietly in the warm sun.

From the corner sofa, behind yesterday's newspaper, Sandra watched Martha open a large pink bag that Sandra had not seen before. Martha reached down inside it and drew out a children's picture book. The print was so large that Sandra could see from the other side of the room that it was on the life of Monet. Martha flicked quickly through until she came to one particular page. She stared at it for some time.

In the morning light Sandra saw that Martha's strawberry blond hair was beginning to grey and that beneath the table one of her small feet was turned inward and resting on top of the other. Martha had good legs for all she was thickish on top—Sandra could see her ankles above the heavy leather sandals and below the hopelessly old-fashioned skirt. She watched Martha's hands, short and plump and stumpy-fingered, resting easily at the edges of the book. Martha had tilted the back up slightly to avoid the reflection of light.

Sandra was studying her so intently that when Martha moved she almost jumped. Martha leaned to the bag on the floor and took out a few balls of wool—lavenders, greens, and pinks, and one bark brown, and arrayed them in line on the table in front of her, referring to the open Monet book. She shifted one ball of wool and then another, like tiles on a Scrabble rack, then leaned back with her hands behind her head and stared at them. A few minutes later she took a strand from each of two adjacent greens, dropped them on the floor, and wound a new ball of double thread. A gradation, Sandra realised, a transition piece, a kind of editing, linking two paragraphs that didn't quite fit. Their crafts were not so different after all.

All day Sandra observed Martha, who was more animated, more engaged, than at any time in the long drive. What was it about Martha she found so fascinating? Her otherness, maybe, and of course her skill and deftness with wool. But what else? Oh, yes, her careless propensity for joy. Martha enjoyed everything: the magpie digging for worms on the front lawn, the tiny delicate bush flowers, the childhood taste of the long green stems of soursobs, the smell of Kate's glycerine soap. She did not appear to own much, or earn much. She had had her own griefs and disappointments. How did she travel so lightly and laugh so easily?

On the first night, after Tony cooked dinner and they finally cleared the table, they played Scrabble. Martha surprised them all with her extensive vocabulary and a cheerfully relentless competitiveness. Sandra had begun the game with a certain discretion, not wanting to show off with obscure words — but when Martha put *quincunx* on a triple word score, using all her letters, the rest of them were obliged to resort to the dictionary. Sandra threw off the traces then and tried to catch up, but it was too late. Kate and Tony were laughing too hard at Sandra's late burst of attention to care about their scores.

"Where did you learn to play like that?" Sandra asked Martha over cocoa and crumpets.

"At home, Sunday afternoons. We had a long-drop dunny out the back, with an old Oxford dictionary hanging from a nail. Malcolm and I learned new words to try and beat Dad. I learned all the *q* words off by heart."

No matter how many times Sandra tried to categorise Martha, she kept turning into something else.

THE second evening, after a day of working on patterns and a leisurely dinner with some smooth red, Sandra suggested they tell stories from their lives before the age of twenty.

"You make everything hard work," complained Tony. "Don't you ever let up?"

"You first," said Sandra. "You're the oldest."

"Let me think," said Tony, leaning back in his chair. "OK. Back when I was a boy, long, long ago . . ." Kate and Sandra rolled their eyes. Martha leaned forward.

"Go on, Tony."

So Tony told how as a fourteen-year-old he and two friends had wagged school and had ridden their bikes down storm-water drains. In the dark he had fallen off his bike and cut his head quite deeply, but he had to wait until school finished to have it stitched, to avoid being found out. Sandra and Kate had heard the story before, but Tony added embellishments for his appreciative new audience. Martha rocked with laughter and applauded every paragraph.

Kate's story began when she was eighteen. Tony had proposed eight times before she said yes. She switched back and forth, replaying the events, mimicking her own youthfulness, her parents, and Tony's increasing desperation. Again, the story was mainly for Martha. The wine loosened them and they laughed easily.

"Now you, Martha," said Tony.

"Well," said Martha, "I'll tell you what happened when I was seventeen. There are things your friends should know." She stood up and smoothed down her clothes and moved so that she was standing in a free space where they could all see her. She patted her hair, made eye contact with each of them in turn, clasped her hands in a melodramatic gesture, and began.

"My name is Martha, make no mistake.

"My name is Martha. I am the sister of Malcolm, and I am seventeen years old. Our father and mother are dead.

"I am Martha the wife of Manny. Martha, Manny and Malcolm. Three Ms in a nice straight row.

"My brother Malcolm is married to Penelope. Penny and I don't get on.

"Manny is dead. This is how I felt the day that Manny died."

Martha sat down and assumed another pose. Sandra looked across at Kate. What was she making of this strange performance?

"Manny's chops are on the plate in the fridge, covered with plastic wrap. I must throw them out. They have been there five days and are starting to smell. I can't bring myself to throw them out, because that is the last thing I did for him, cook those chops. It was a mistake to cook them so early: even if he had come home they would have been tough as leather. I am still learning how to time the cooking so everything ends up perfectly all at once, and nobody is waiting for the potato to mash or the gravy to be made. It's not Manny who cares, it's me. Manny likes everything, including me." Here Martha winked heavily. "And I like Manny too. But I like to have everything just right."

Martha sighed heavily and went on. Her voice filled the room.

"Manny rides his bike to work and on the way home someone knocks him off. He never came home to eat those chops. At the funeral it is freezing and rains. I wear his leather jacket over the jumper I made him. They are much too big, of course, but it is like going with him, only it's his funeral, so how can I be going with him? I can't think straight. I can't breathe properly. I have been knitting, because knitting helps me breathe. I am knitting a scarf. It's too long, it's ten feet long, but I can't stop, it just keeps growing, and I just keep adding more wool." Martha's hands were busy showing and shaping.

"What would happen if I stopped? That's the question. I have rolled the scarf up from the bottom and pinned it with nappy pins. We won't be needing them for a baby, not now, because you can't have a baby without a father. The scarf gets longer and longer. I must stop soon, I must stop knitting and throw out those chops."

Kate and Sandra exchanged looks. What had they unleashed? Was it finished? But Martha went on.

"I'm making a weeping scarf, a mourning scarf. A mourning scarf to wear on a cold morning. I will knit it long enough to wrap around the house. The house and I will stay wrapped up forever with memories of Manny. But I can't keep the chops forever, or I won't be able to stay in the house.

"Where is my knitting? I made a mistake. I must fix the mistake so I can knit and keep calm, so I don't make more mistakes. It's a love scarf to keep me warm, there's no mistake about that. My name is Martha. Thank you."

Martha bowed and sat down in her chair. The performance was over. Neither Sandra nor Kate knew what to say, but Tony laughed suddenly.

"So did you throw out the chops?"

"Of course I did," said Martha in her ordinary voice. "You can't keep going like that, keeping yourself and your chops wrapped up forever. Besides, they started to stink."

"And did you really knit a scarf big enough to go around the house?"

Martha grinned. "No, but it was pretty long! I could wrap it around myself a few times."

"And did it work? Knitting it? Did it really keep you calm?"

"Yes. But then I made a lot of mistakes and things got messy. But Malcolm organised a holiday for me. I got better eventually."

Sandra and Kate were silent. Normal rules did not apply. Tony, never known for his conversational sensitivity, was holding everything together.

"Have you still got the scarf?"

Martha frowned.

"Somewhere. Tucked away."

"I'd like to see it," said Tony.

"No way," said Martha. "I don't show people my mistakes. I bet you don't either."

"Good one!" said Tony. "No, I don't." He paused. "Well, thanks, Martha, that was very interesting. Glass of port, anyone? Or a cup of tea? Then it's your turn, Sandra."

"Oh, we've had enough, haven't we?" said Sandra. "Martha gave a real performance. I couldn't do anything like that." She saw the pain on Martha's face. "I mean, it's getting late. We should be going to bed."

"Oh, no, you don't," said Tony. "You started this. We've all had a turn. Don't think you can dip out, just because you're a poor old widow."

"Tony!" said Kate.

"You don't mind, do you, Sandy?" Tony was the only person in the world who could get away with calling her that. And Sandra didn't mind his teasing. It was better than everyone tiptoeing around her feelings all the time.

So Tony brewed tea in the white china pot and poured them each a cup. They all looked at Sandra expectantly. Well, she'd tell them something they hadn't heard before.

"When I was a kid," said Sandra, "I was staying with Aunty Mert. My mother had been sick and my dad was being a misery, so Aunty Mert took me to her place for a few days. On Saturday morning I came out for breakfast, and there she was dressed up in her good clothes.

" 'Are you going out?' I said. Yes, she was.

" 'Where?' I asked her.

" 'Got some business,' she said. 'But Uncle Darce is

taking you to the beach with the cousins.' There were five of us, and we often went to the beach.

"So I packed my beach bag, but I knew something was odd. Aunty Mert wouldn't look at me. I said I'd wait out the front for Uncle Darce.

"As I was going down the hall she called me back and knelt down so her face was level with mine.

" 'Listen, kiddo,' she said. 'I can't tell you what I'm doing today because the family won't let me. Otherwise I would. One day you'll work it all out. And when you do, just remember I thought you should come with us and not go to the beach.'

" 'But I want to go to the beach,' I said

" 'Good,' she said. 'You just enjoy it. I hope you have a very happy day.'

"Anyway, we played on the beach all morning. Then, when we were sitting on the rug under the jetty having lunch, my oldest cousin said, 'How come you're not at the funeral?'

" 'What funeral?' I asked.

" 'Your mother's,' he said.

"She'd died, you know, and they hadn't even told me. Nobody had told me. Aunty Mert was the youngest aunt, and the others wouldn't let her tell me. They didn't want me at the funeral, so they decided they'd wait until after."

The others sat in respectful silence. Tony proffered the pot of tea, Sandra nodded, Tony poured. There was a sniff from Martha's chair, and then another.

Martha was crying, her face heavy with tears, a large hanky held to her nose. Her shoulders were shaking. The other three looked at one another in consternation. Martha kept crying, quietly and thoroughly, then put her head down on the arm of her padded chair and began to sob loudly, with small cries of pain that increased in volume as time went on. Wailing, thought Sandra. Martha is wailing.

"Martha," said Sandra, "whatever's the matter?"

More sobs.

"Did I say something to upset you?" Sandra was quickly reviewing her own story, and Martha's. Was Martha unstable? Had she said too much?

Sandra looked at Kate and Tony, then got out of her chair and went to kneel by Martha, putting a tentative hand on her shoulder.

"Martha? Are you all right?"

"I'm all right," said Martha, looking Sandra full in the face. They searched each other's eyes. Martha's face was red and blubbery like a child's.

"I'm all right," she repeated. "It's you I'm crying for, Sandra." She swiped at her running nose. "Because you can't. You don't know how."

Sandra sat back on her heels. Then she picked up her cup of tea and took it out into the night.

SANDRA and Kate had had enough sightseeing, but Tony had a list and wanted to visit everything, as did Martha.

They had climbed through caves, gawked at the Blue Lake, toured the pumping station, done the boardwalk, stared into the still deep water of Ewens Ponds. Now they pulled into yet another car park.

Kate eyed the sandy hill. "I'm staying here, Tony. But take your time."

Sandra took out her binoculars to look at birds and said she'd keep Kate company.

Tony and Martha trudged up the hill. It wasn't as hard going as it looked, though they were glad to pause at the top. The beach stretched for miles, a long white expanse in both directions, the tide halfway.

"This way, I reckon," said Tony, turning left. Martha stopped to take off her shoes. Her springy hair had gone wild in the wind, and her skirt flapped around her bare legs.

Tony enjoyed Martha's company. She loved everything, the ink-black caves, the startling blue of Blue Lake, the hollowed volcanic shell of Mount Schank. At the bottom of the empty crater she had written MARTHA WAS HERE with white stones, and read the words from the top of the ridge with great satisfaction. Taking Martha around was like having an excited child for company, which allowed Tony to return freshly himself when he was in danger of being disappointed by finding beloved places diminished or slicked over for tourists. Yesterday he had seen the yawning mouth of a cave that had been accessible in his youth; now it was gated and locked against him and the torch he had packed in anticipation.

Martha had tucked her skirt into her knickers and was prancing along the beach waving her arms in the air. She looked like a large flapping kite that couldn't quite take off. Tony tried to swing his arms as he walked along and clapped his hands once or twice, but he felt like a dancing bear. He couldn't quite bring himself to cavort. Sandra might be watching through her binoculars from a sand hill.

"Tony! Look!"

Martha had stopped still and was staring at a spot in front of her feet. Next to her knobby toes, water was erupting out of the flat sand like a miniature volcano.

"What is it? Oh, no! The wave's covered it."

She waited anxiously for the water to ebb.

As it receded, Tony saw it, too, the clear bright water bubbling out of beach sand.

"There's more, Tony—look! There! And there!" Martha was spinning around, pointing and laughing.

All around were little craters of bubbling sand. Yes, this was it. And this time just as he remembered. Tony bent down and cupped his hand in the water.

"Taste it." He smiled and put his mouth to his hand.

Martha dipped her fingers in one of the holes and licked them.

"What? It's fresh!" Martha looked so surprised that Tony laughed out loud.

"But how come?"

"It's a freshwater spring."

"We nearly walked right past! We nearly missed it! We would have if the tide was higher."

For a few minutes they watched the miracle of fresh water flowing through persistent washes of salt.

"I want to see how deep they are. Here, Tony, hold my hand."

Tony held out a steadying hand while Martha swayed, awkward and unbalanced, her foot deep in one of the bubbling craters.

"It's rocky down the bottom. Like broken shells."

She let go of Tony. "I want to put my hand in."

Martha leaned over and put her hand down as far as she could reach, threatening to topple.

"Watch out, you'll get wet."

"But I want to feel the bottom."

"You did, with your foot."

She ignored him, waited till the wave receded again, then knelt on the sand, pushing her hand deep down so that the water bubbled above her elbow.

"It's stony. Like broken rock. I think there's one big hole and lots of little holes, but I can't tell, because of the shells and stones."

"You're going to get wet."

But it was too late. A wave swirled around Martha, up and over her legs, lifting her skirt around her like a hooped petticoat. She gasped with the shock of it. Tony offered her his hand, but Martha sat back in the water and laughed uproariously. Then, to Tony's dismay, she kicked out her legs, turned over, and lay full-length, front side down, in the water. The sea flowed away, leaving her marooned on the sand like a small beached whale. She put her face down to the spring and drank greedily.

"It's good, Tony! Want some? You get more this way."

"No, thanks."

"You don't know what you're missing."

"Yes, I do. I'm missing wet and cold all the way home."

"Tastes really good. I was thirsty." She splashed water at him. Tony moved out of reach, uncomfortable. He started back toward the car.

Martha trailed behind. Her legs chafed against her wet clothes. She saw a black double fin sweeping along, fishing close to shore, but she didn't tell Tony—he was too far away. It was dangerous out here. You had to watch out. Anything could happen.

Behind the security of Tony's determined back she slipped off her wet undies and wrung them out. She wouldn't embarrass him if she could help it. She put them in one of her big skirt pockets. Sand rasped her skin in awkward places. It had been worth it though, to feel that deep and secret water bubbling up hard against her body and have the cool fresh water washing her mouth.

IN THE car, Kate and Sandra had been talking.

"Martha's strong, you know," said Sandra. "She's really robust. You wouldn't think it to look at her, but she is."

"Why do you say that?"

"Imagine, a young woman, and her husband killed like that. Sure, sounds like she was pretty disturbed at the time, but she moved through it OK. She's never remarried; she's quite content to live her single life, be responsible for herself. She's not grieving. She might have been weak once, but now she's as tough as an old boot."

"Everyone's got their vulnerabilities," said Kate. "Maybe you just don't know Martha well enough."

But Sandra had made up her mind. "No, she's a healthy survivor. I wish I was strong like her."

"You're too hard on yourself," said Kate. "Jack's only been gone twelve months."

At that point Martha and Tony opened the doors and climbed in. Martha leaned toward Sandra as she reached around for her seat belt.

"Ugh! Martha, you're all wet. What did you do, go swimming?"

Martha's skin was blotched purple with cold.

"No, I got baptised."

"You are really weird, Martha," said Sandra, then bit her tongue.

"Yes," said Martha cheerfully. "Just like you." She

turned to look at Sandra. "Only your trouble is you don't know how to enjoy it."

Like a child, Sandra gave Martha a little shove. Martha pushed her back, gently, but with a lot of body contact, so that a good deal of wetness was transferred.

"She's wetting me, Mum," complained Sandra to Kate.

"Stop fighting, you two," said Kate. "Martha, move over to your side of the car. Does anyone want a Mintie?"

"Yes," said Tony. He chewed it stoically, looking straight ahead over the steering wheel, pretending to ignore the commotion in the back seat.

On their fourth night Kate said, "We're going out to dinner."

"Good," said Sandra. "Time for a change. Where shall we go?"

"No, Sandra. 'We' as in Tony and me. We need time out."

"Oops. Sorry. Sure. Of course you do." And off they went.

Sandra and Martha waved them goodbye from the door like forlorn parents waving off a honeymoon couple.

At eight o'clock the phone rang. It was Kate. They'd had a few drinks and didn't want to drive. They were staying in a motel. Sandra, who had never known Kate to have more than two glasses of wine, found this hard to believe.

She and Martha had a counterpoint dinner of baked beans on toast.

"Beans, beans, they're good for the heart, beans, beans, they make you fart," said Martha.

"I'm going for a walk on the beach," said Sandra with an edge to her voice.

"Shall I come?"

"No, I'd rather go by myself if you don't mind."

"Sure. No worries. Just like Kate and Tony," said Martha. "But at least I asked."

"What do you mean?"

"Well, we weren't really invited on this holiday, were we? But here we are, cooped up together like a batch of new chickens. We need a bit of space, I reckon. I'm going for a walk too, but I'll go the other way. All right?"

Sandra would have preferred the whole beach to herself. As she walked, with Martha far in the distance, she tried to figure out whether Martha was right. Had she been invited on this week away, or had she presumed? She honestly couldn't remember.

Sandra went for a long walk, around the spit and back. When she returned to the house, Martha was working on her strange white garment. She packed it up when Sandra came in the door.

"Don't stop."

"No, it's OK. I've had enough. Do you want to start looking at those patterns?"

They got out Sandra's filing box and the flat leather

school case with the collection of wartime pattern books. Martha had also brought a few patterns of her own.

"Shonger bonger, look at this," said Martha. "Nineteen eighteen, Khaki Comforts! Soldiers' stuff. Balaclava with cape pieces. Looks like it should be made of chain mail. What are those big flappy bits for? To protect his chest?"

"Yes, you had to keep your chest warm. Flu epidemics, remember. And no proper heating." Sandra turned the page. "Look, here's another variety. It's even called a chest protector."

"Looks like an undershirt," said Martha. "Only too short. That would never keep his bum warm. What are those little tabs at the waist? Oh, I see," she said, running her finger down the lines of pattern. "There's no side seam. It's like a tabard. Well, that wouldn't be much good either, letting the drafts in like that."

"And here," said Sandra, "we have knee caps, an abdominal band, a body belt, a naval jersey, and a lady's cape."

"Is there a picture of the cape?"

"No, just the pattern. I think it must have been on the cover, which has torn off."

"It's a nice pattern," said Martha, reading through it. "Flared from the shoulders, with hand holes, and a seam down the center so it keeps its shape. I wouldn't mind making that one. What date is it?"

"Nineteen twenty-one."

"Do you want that one?"

"Yes," said Sandra, grabbing the opportunity. "What about these war things that were sent to the soldiers in the trenches?"

"They're easy. Even you could knit them. Only take a night or two each."

"No, I'm the word person, you're the knitter. I'd mess them up."

"You could learn. I'd teach you."

"No," said Sandra. "Can't do it."

"Won't, you mean," said Martha.

"All right. Won't. I know my limitations. And I don't want to. Besides, I have to organise other things. I've been looking everywhere, and I still haven't been able to find an exhibition space."

"You could use the church hall," said Martha.

"So we could! Those lovely polished floorboards. I wonder what it would cost."

"Not much. Ask Kate. She'll probably get it for you for free." Martha smoothed down the yellowing pattern in front of her and sighed. A hall full of garments. It was going to be a big job.

ON THE coastal drive back to Adelaide, just before the town of Robe, the wind picked up. It was warm in the car, but the minute they stepped out in front of the bakery they knew they wanted hot food for lunch. They pushed aside the plastic strips hanging in the doorway and trooped in.

"Mm," said Tony, "steak and kidney pie. I'll have one of those, and a sausage roll, and a buttered finger bun, thanks."

Kate patted him on the tummy.

"Not good for you, Tony."

"Holidays," he said. "And a carton of chocolate milk, please."

Kate shook her head. She and Sandra each chose an oversized samosa.

"What are you having, Martha?" said Sandra, watching her count coins.

"Don't know yet."

"Another samosa, please," said Sandra to the woman taking the orders. "Put your purse away, Martha, my treat."

Tony paid for himself and Kate, Sandra paid the rest. She bought Martha an orange juice as well.

They went down to the wharf for lunch. A flock of seagulls squawked and squabbled.

"Look," said Martha, "that one has only one leg."

"Must have been bitten by a shark," said Tony.

Martha threw a large chunk of samosa to the maimed gull, which caught it deftly and flew off.

"Nothing wrong with its wings, at any rate," said Tony.

Sandra's attention was on another gull, at the far edge

of the crowd, darting in for food but never quite getting it. Martha also saw it and threw another large piece of samosa in its direction. Again the gull missed out.

"Are you eating any of that?" asked Sandra sharply.

"Not much," Martha said. "Don't like curry. And I'm allergic to orange juice. Do you want it?"

"You should have said."

"You didn't give me a chance," said Martha. "I wanted a pastie."

"You should stick up for yourself," said Sandra crossly. "How am I supposed to know these things?"

There was not much talking on the last leg home. A week together had been long enough.

BACK in her study Sandra tenderly took the 1945 baby's pattern book out of its plastic sleeve. It was printed on wartime paper, fraying at the edges, the pages bound together with thread, and faint pencil marks in a margin showed where someone had kept track of the pattern. The price was two shillings.

On the front cover was a black-and-white photo of a seated baby that looked like the life-sized doll Sandra had had as a child, with its legs stuck out in front and a round, chubby, expressionless face under a bonnet that hid its hair and its personality. The unsmiling baby was dressed in layers: a dress, a longish matinee jacket, matching bootees and mittens. An insert in the corner showed what it was wearing underneath: a ribbed undershirt with a gathering ribbon at the neck and a pair of knitted pants with a similar drawstring at the waist. The set of patterns on the cover was called starfish and was knitted in a shell pattern, with scallops at the hem.

At the beginning of the pattern was a list of the notions necessary to make the layette: eight 1-ounce balls of two-ply wool, a pair each of number 12 and 14 needles, a darning needle, six buttons, half a yard of narrow ribbon, one size 12 crochet hook. The pattern instructions read like some kind of code. Sandra looked for the legend and translated the abbreviations, but there were no diagrams, and she couldn't make proper sense of it. Too hard. This wasn't her field anyway.

This was one of Martha's books. She put it in her own brand of plastic sleeve, then in the ring binder, numbering the corner with a small self-stick label and updating the filing page with Martha's name and address and a brief description.

After putting it on the shelf, she remembered that Martha would need a copy, so she took it out again to run through the photocopier. She folded the copied pages into an envelope—much bulkier than the original—and addressed it to Martha. She didn't want to call on her again. She'd had enough of Martha for a couple of weeks. Besides, Martha probably just wanted to get on with the job.

❦

MARTHA saw the yellow envelope sticking up out of the mailbox and went out to see what it was. It had the university logo on it. Inside was a copy of her pattern, from Sandra, with a brief note.

> Dear Martha, I'd like to keep this for a while, but I know you need the instructions. Here's a copy to keep you going. Yours, Sandra.

No *please*, no *would you mind*, no *love*, either. Martha had not expected Sandra to keep the pattern—she hadn't said she would. The photocopy paper was not the same. It was brazenly white, and thick, with a hard edge, and printed on only one side, so it wasted paper. And it was new, as though nobody had ever used this pattern before, when in fact that pattern book had been used to dress three generations of McKenzies, the last being Malcolm's grandson.

One page was crooked and the page number missing. The photo of the baby was a grey blur, so you couldn't see how the shell pattern was supposed to look. Poor little starfish baby, dressed in those hot clothes under the photographer's bright lights. She had a blank look on her face. Perhaps she was thirsty and wanting a drink.

Martha read easily through the pattern Sandra wanted, noting a discrepancy here and there where the pattern maker had made a mistake. The eleventh row of the pattern repeat would need counting: Martha hadn't done anything quite like it before, though it was easy enough to read and shouldn't be a problem. If she'd had the original she could have had a good look at the photo to see just what the effect of that row would be, but now she'd have to knit it to find out. Although she preferred to see it, there was a certain pleasure in working without the photo, like doing a jigsaw without the picture on the box. Two-ply wool was very fine. Did Sandra want it in wool? Nylon might be better; it didn't irritate soft baby skin, although that new machine-washable baby wool might be all right. No, you'd never get it in two-ply, not these days. Martha didn't fancy splitting several balls of four-ply either. That would take hours, and it probably wouldn't work.

But Sandra would want wool for it, to be authentic 1945, and indeed Martha had several bags of suitable two-ply white wool. But that was special, the wool she was using for the roseheart dress.

She had a few odd balls of cream that she and Sandra had picked up on their thrift-shop crawl. That was fairly old — perhaps it would do. Martha went to look. Yes, there was enough, though it was the wrong ply. She rang Sandra.

"You know that baby's layette, the old one? Do you mind if it's in three-ply?"

"What's it supposed to be?"

"Two."

"It would be better to have what the pattern calls for."

Silence.

"Sure you haven't got an old bag of two-ply stashed away somewhere?"

There was a long pause.

"Well, I have, but it's spoken for."

More silence. Martha could hear Sandra gathering herself for a push, and got in first.

"You'll hardly notice the difference." Martha braced herself for the assault.

"Could you get some more somewhere?"

"Maybe, but it's hard to come by, that stuff. It's special." No, Sandra, please don't insist. Please don't. You'll spoil everything.

"Can't be that hard. It's a big country."

Martha stayed miserably silent. She knew she wasn't strong enough to hold out against Sandra; if Sandra kept on about it, Martha would blow over like grass in the wind, and that would spoil everything. Help me, somebody, don't let Sandra spoil things for herself.

Sandra, listening, was too impatient to wait and abruptly changed her mind.

"All right, then, if you think the three-ply won't matter and you can adjust the pattern. I don't suppose anyone will know except you. But Martha, I thought you liked everything exactly right. It doesn't seem consistent—you, of all people, using the wrong ply."

"I do like everything right, that's true. I like the pattern to be absolutely perfect. But every knitter is different. You always have to do a tension square. The things you work with, the size needles and the wool, and any adjustments you have to make, that's up to you. You make up your mind what it's supposed to be, and then you do it. Perfectly."

Sandra's mind was racing ahead beyond these technicalities. "OK, Martha, I'll leave it to you. You're the expert."

"At least I'll be able to get on with it, because I've got it here already. And we need to do that order. The new sample cards from the yarn suppliers have all arrived."

It had not occurred to Sandra that wool might have to be ordered.

"Can't we get it locally?"

"No, there's only a couple of decent wool shops around here, and the woollen mill up in the hills, but they don't always have what you want. Ordering direct is the quickest way. You don't have to wait until the shop puts in an order. You can find the wholesalers on the Internet and ring direct."

So Martha was Net savvy, even though she didn't have a computer. Another surprise. They arranged a time to look at the sample cards and hung up.

Martha needed a cup of tea. She stirred the sugar in slowly, listening to the clinking spoon change pitch as the sugar dissolved. That had been a close shave. The white wool was spoken for, but Sandra, like a child, wanted everything *now*.

ON PENSION day Cliff stood in line at the newsagent and waited. There was a new girl behind the counter in a tight red T-shirt. Martha never wore T-shirts, she always wore button-up blouses. Cliff didn't know which he liked better, the clinging stretch of bright red or the tease of buttons. Not that Martha ever gave him a chance, but she couldn't stop him from thinking about it, no harm in that. *She's beautiful, and therefore to be woo'd; She is a woman, therefore to be won.* Now Sandra was another matter. If you even thought about stretching out a finger to Sandra, she would bite it off. Besides, she probably wore a bloody bulletproof vest. Not that she had anything to show. Unlike Martha, who was nice and round and soft.

Cliff always prayed on pension day. He prayed three times. The first prayer was at the newsagent's, that he would pick the best scratchie. The second was in the food line, where he had a choice of pie, hot dogs or hamburger, that he'd get a big serving. The third prayer was the grace remembered from some obscure corner of childhood: *For what we are about to receive may the Lord make us truly thankful.*

That way, if you didn't win the scratchie, you kept your options open with The Bloke Upstairs. The big win would come when it was meant.

January

MARTHA TOOK advantage of the air conditioning in Sandra's car and worked on the lady's cape all the way to the woollen mill. Normally she didn't knit wool in the heat of summer, but Sandra wanted the exhibition in May, only seventeen weeks away. Martha was feeling pushed before she had barely begun. She didn't understand Sandra's urgency, why the exhibition had to fill every nook and cranny of Sandra's life, and now every nook and cranny of her own. Why couldn't it be later in the year? But when she had suggested a postponement Sandra had said no, that later on her students would be more stressed, and she'd be busy with marking, and organising some conference, and finishing a collaborative book. Martha had nothing to offer in the face of such argument except a sense of dread, so she said nothing. The exhibition would be in May. That was that.

As they entered the car park she unclipped her seat belt. Before Sandra had turned off the engine, Martha had grabbed her handbag from the floor and was getting out. She leaned back inside briefly.

"I'll see you in there." And she was off, almost running, toward the blue door under the big square letters of WOOL SALES.

Martha had not been to the mill for several years, as it was not accessible by public transport. Instead she had relied on the sample cards that came each quarter, tufted with that season's range of colours and textures. Martha's delight in a new card had been a revelation to Sandra — she had seen how Martha's eyes lit up when she took it from the mailbox, and how, during their shared coffee in Martha's tidy kitchen, she had opened and reopened the card, running her finger down the samples, bending the card a little to juxtapose particular colours.

"Look at those sea colours," she had said. "They're new this year. They are so beautiful! See, this dark one for the deep water, and that pale greeny one for the sandbars. I'd use those, and that one called driftwood, but then I'd get this other one as well." She turned the card over. "That soft one there — mulberry — because it's like a stormy sunset. You know, when you have a big purple cloud, right at that golden time before the sun sets." Sandra did know, and could see how well the colours looked together, though such a mix would never have occurred to her.

As Sandra entered the shop, Martha looked up and

gave her an open-faced, happy smile. She was like a child in a toy shop. She turned back to inspect a bank of greens: olive, jade, leaf, kiwi, lime, a silver-green like the back of birch leaves, a bright pistachio. Martha couldn't look without touching. She picked up the huge hanks one by one, feeling their weight, inspecting the degree of twist, testing the strength.

Then another sign caught her eye.

"Oh, the bargain room!" and she was off to the back, burrowing through tea chests and wire baskets.

"What are you looking for, exactly?" asked Sandra, coming alongside, the list of necessities she and Martha had compiled fluttering feebly from one hand.

"Nothing," said Martha cheerfully. "Just seeing what's here. Just having a big fat look. Oh, Sandra!" She straightened suddenly and grabbed Sandra in a big bear hug. "Thank you for bringing me here! Thank you! Thank you! You are so kind to me."

Sandra found a basket and tried to assemble the things they needed, but she couldn't do it. She didn't have Martha's colour sense, and she didn't know enough about wool. She would just have to wait until Martha had finished. She tried to relax and enjoy the display, to get some sense of what Martha saw and felt, but whatever it was that enthralled Martha escaped her. Only one bin really attracted her attention; after assessing everything on the basis of cost, she was drawn back to the luxury oddments, and in particular a few balls of a yarn called sunshower, pale blue with silver flecks.

She held it next to her face in the mirror and suddenly saw Martha's face behind her. Sandra flushed a little.

"That would be all right," Martha said. "But how about this?" And she picked out several other balls.

"See, amethyst, violet, plum, this wonderful rich dark gold, and" — her hand hovered for a moment and then darted in — "this one!" She held up a deep green and squinted at the label.

"Coppermine! See how good and strong they are, how they balance each other?" She stood behind Sandra so they could both see in the mirror and framed her head with the different-coloured balls, a woolly coronet.

"Beautiful, with your dark hair. A real statement! What are you going to make?"

Sandra felt shy. "Oh, nothing much. Just a scarf or something. I'm not very good at knitting."

"I'll show you."

"Are you ready yet? Shall we get the exhibition wool?"

"Oh, yes!" Martha laughed. "I nearly forgot. That's why we came. Where's the list? It won't take long."

Nor did it. In fifteen minutes Martha had gathered the wool for a dozen garments. Sandra took out her Visa card and prepared to pay, while Martha fossicked in her bag for her purse.

"No, you don't have to pay anything, Martha, don't be silly."

"Yes, I do," said Martha, "because they won't let me take this lot out for free." She pointed to three baskets already behind the counter. "That's all mine. Not for the exhibition, just for myself. Three weeks worth of pension I've got there."

On the way home Sandra asked, "What sort of pension are you on?"

"Oh, I'm not really. We just call it that. Family joke. I inherited a share of the farm, and I've got a deal with Malcolm. Some years it's good, and other years it's not much. Malcolm takes care of me, even if his wife has ants in her pants."

"All that wool you bought—you're not going to knit that up before the exhibition, are you?"

"First things first," said Martha, picking up the round needle she was using for the cape. Though her voice was reassuring, Sandra wasn't sure that her first and Martha's first were the same thing.

MARTHA was an early riser, an old habit learned on the farm that had calcified into her bones. After the usual routine of breakfast, dishes and sweeping, she went to her workroom. Yesterday she had taken all the wool out of its flimsy plastic bags and put it in baskets—the exhibition wool in a utilitarian plastic laundry basket, but her own wool in two ancient wicker baskets that had been passed down through two or three generations on her mother's side. She had pushed mothballs in among the skeins like seeds in the ground. The room smelled delicious.

But before starting on the exhibition pieces, Martha took down the calico bag hanging from a hook on the back of the door and opened out the secret white garment she was making in two-ply lambswool, the wool Sandra had wanted for the baby's layette. She had been lucky to come by that wool. She held up the bodice, which was almost finished, and viewed it with a critical eye. It was good, very good, perhaps the most beautiful thing she had ever made. Flawless, and the rose pattern was just right. And it should fit, too.

For the next hour she worked away at the rose pattern. This too was habit, this hour at the beginning of the day before her other work, this hour set aside for love and pleasure. When she first began this quiet time, she had listened to the radio, but after a while she found that she preferred silence, to sit still and peacefully think things through while her hands moved easy on the needles. Sometimes she felt another presence, someone comfortable and caring. This work was different from the rest; this work gave more than it took, strengthened her somehow. Like dipping into a well. And it was peaceful. No one was likely to ring before seven in the morning.

This was the time when she had her best ideas. Only

a few minutes before, she had decided to change the pattern for the skirt of this new dress. The bodice, almost finished now, was all in roseheart pattern, but she wanted something different for the skirt, something that would draw the eye upward. Feather stitch, that would be perfect. The lambswool would soften and slightly blur the elongated rows of paired holes. She could put each row of feathers slightly off-centre from the previous row, so that the skirt would hint at the idea of a folded wing. Roseheart for the bodice, feather stitch for the skirt and sleeves, with bands of roseheart at the hem and cuffs for balance. She would need a multiple of seven stitches to begin the skirt. For weeks she had searched and thought, feeling her way toward the form, and now the sense of the whole had crept quietly into her mind when she was least expecting it. Martha's heart leapt with recognition. She was so excited she put down her knitting and for a few minutes walked around waving her arms in the air to settle herself down.

Sandra could do with a bit of this, thought Martha, starting a new row. Sandra was always pulled out tight, like a rubber band ready for pinging. She could do with a bit of comfort knitting in the morning. But Sandra was a night person; she always slept late. Perhaps Sandra's hour needed to be at the end of the day, under the moon.

Martha worked steadily, without mistakes, until the hour was up. Time to stand and stretch for a while. And then she must have another go at the lady's cape, to see if she could fix that mistake she had made in the car. After that she would start that man's funny bathing suit. Fancy actually wearing anything like that, and getting it wet! Martha's skin felt irritated just thinking about it.

THE phone rang. Sandra, stepping out of the shower and towelling her hair, nearly missed it.

"Sandra Fildes?"

"Speaking."

"My name's Jonty Stewart? New Zealand? You may not remember me, but I was at the Wollongong conference?" She ended each sentence with an irritating upward inflection. Sandra remembered the keynote speaker, a soft-bodied woman in her mid-forties with startling pink glasses frames.

"I heard you were mounting a retro knitting exhibition. I'm writing a book called *Stitching the Empire*. I'd like to come over for the opening if I can." Sandra suddenly saw herself, stark naked except for a towel around her head, talking to Dr Stewart, the internationally known writer on postcolonial textiles.

Her little exhibition had taken on a life of its own.

CLIFF put his scratchy to one side, spread out the paper napkin and tucked it under his clean-shaven chin. Pension day was also shaving day and shower day. Of course you couldn't quite go from one pension day to the next without a shower—two weeks was a long time. Your resources might be limited, but you could always keep yourself clean. A bucket of water went a long way.

Today there were only three people in front of him when he lined up to buy the ticket. That was lucky. Odd numbers were lucky, and prime numbers were especially lucky. Three was very lucky. Thirteen was the luckiest number of all, but not many people believed that.

Cliff took a bite of his hot dog. Mustard spurted unexpectedly but landed on his napkin. There you go, lucky day. He chewed the rest slowly; he was missing a few back teeth, which didn't make for speed. And he knew from experience that swallowing without chewing was not a good idea. As he chewed, he stared at the unscratched ticket, enjoying the anticipation. What was under that silver surface? Maybe only a couple of dollars. He'd won two dollars seven weeks ago; since then, nothing. His luck was definitely due to come in. This time it would be the big one.

The hot dog was finished, the milk reduced to a few bubbles. Cliff folded his napkin into rectangle, square, triangle. He opened his wallet and took out his lucky two-cent piece, kept from the old days. Under the first silver square was a heart. Then a chicken, a dog and a feather. And two fish. It was depressing. Maybe he'd used up all the luck he was ever going to get.

SANDRA sat in her study writing the labels to accompany Martha's garments. As usual, she had far too much material, enough for a book actually, which she had to condense down to one video, one interactive display, two information panels and thirty-seven small notations to accompany the garments.

Too many words again. The old dilemma — quantitative or qualitative — and the need to balance the two. And the need to stay aware of her own biases, question her own motives.

Why couldn't she just relax? Did it really matter if she unwittingly subverted her own purpose? Or some other purpose, for that matter, something beyond and bigger than herself?

Yes, it most certainly did. You had to stay in control. If you didn't know exactly what you were doing, you could be caught out.

Martha was lucky. All Martha had to do was read the pattern and follow it. Pure mechanics. Whereas she, Sandra, had to *think* and *decide* and *be responsible*. And of course, *the buck stopped here*. Well, there weren't that many bucks this time, but what there were had to be well and truly answered for.

Even today, when she was doing work she enjoyed, at a subterranean level she was searching, questioning, trying to pin down her own motives. Why was war so fascinating? Time and again she found herself drawn back to the two world wars. Maybe, after losing Jack, she had a morbid fascination with death. Or was it related to her family history, the bundle of letters her grandfather had sent back from France to his new wife? Perhaps it had more to do with her father, his six years of meticulously kept war diary, her memory of him coming out of the shed one day dressed in his old uniform found in a trunk when he'd been looking for something else. And the rough comfort of the khaki picnic rug that he kept in the back of the car, wrapped around her after she'd fallen in the river.

Maybe it wasn't her father. Maybe it was that fascinating community of women, clicking away at their socks and undershirts and balaclavas in church, at the movies, over cups of tea, knitting thousands of small items to be sent to sons and brothers and sweethearts, or to young men they'd never met but might one day when the war was over. And the stoic humor of tough times — *Thanks Aunty for the socks. One of them keeps my feet warm at night, and the other makes a great scarf.*

The past fascinated her, but she couldn't climb back into it, find out what made it tick, just what it was exactly that fired up the older women when they reminisced about ration coupons and blackouts, two-day honeymoons after weddings in borrowed dresses, Americans with good manners and silk stockings. She could only stare at relics and listen to old songs like "Pick Up Your Knitting" on wheezy gramophone records and try to understand the implications of a pattern book called *Knit for Victory*. Maybe there weren't any great secrets. Maybe she just longed for a broader experience, for real community.

Sandra pushed the keyboard away and leaned back in her chair. Her notes sounded false. She opened a folder of primary references. Yes, this was better:

> We began hearing a lot about "the war effort" and people stopped saying the war would be over in six months, or even a year. Whenever I came home from school, the house was full of women clicking knitting needles and manipulating dark wool, and making huge quantities of socks, vests, mittens and mufflers, as well as sewing pyjamas and shirts . . .
> Nora Pennington, the good little girl who had written the composition about Gallipoli, was the school's champion sock knitter. At lunchtime and recess she sat with her ankles neatly crossed and her boots buttoned, turning the heels of the socks very prettily. She eventually won the district record for the number of socks, mufflers, mittens and balaclava helmets knitted by anybody under the age of thirteen; her father made sure that the news reached the front page of his paper, with the heading "LITTLE NORA DOES HER BIT." The rest of us longed to grab her knitting, rip the stitches out and snarl the wool for her. (David Gleason, "At First I Thought it Was the Most Wonderful Adventure", in Jacqueline

Kent, *In the Half Light* [Angus & Robertson, Sydney, 1988], pp. 56–58)

Sandra knew, even as she attached the reference, why she liked that piece. She recognised a kinship with little Nora sitting there knitting with her boots crossed, ordering her world, disciplined and useful, striving for excellence. But she also identified with David Gleason, wanting to rip it all to bits.

THE matinee jacket would not come right.

Martha could feel the flush of anxiety rising from deep down in her belly, rising like a flood to carry her mind away from its moorings into a swirling, panicking fright, bumpy with recollections of getting things wrong. Misjudgement, misplaced trust, not being able to do what was needed, being young and clumsy and stupid—so stupid not to see it coming, not to get it right the first time and avert disaster. She was an idiot, a klutz, a throwaway rag. It was no use, no use at all now, she would never be able to fix it.

But she couldn't throw away all that good wool. What a waste. It was wicked to waste. She would put it in the bag and do it later, do it when she had more time, wasn't busy, do it some never-never day when she was relaxed and able to think clearly, when she could sit down calmly and do what was needed.

She unzipped the big striped bag and thrust the pieces of the jacket as far down as they would go. Baa, baa, black sheep, have you any wool? Yes sir, yes sir, three bags full of mistakes. So many mistakes to carry around all the time, waiting for the right moment when her head was clear and she could think like a normal person and just count the numbers and get it right. That was all it was, some careful unpicking, and counting numbers, and getting it right. But it wasn't a job she could do today. She zipped up the big bag and put it back against the wall. The third bag was nearly full. She couldn't start a fourth bag. Carrying four bags around all the time would kill her.

But that rose dress, that was all right, there were no mistakes in that.

She had better start one of those other things for Sandra.

MINT — that was the colour. Mint green, fresh as mouthwash. The little green dress frolicked at the end of the sales rack, shiny and beautiful, a bright emerald in a dull day. Jack had liked Sandra in green — good for her brown eyes, he said, and a foil for her hair — back in the days when she'd allowed it to be red. Jack had liked being married to a redhead.

It fitted too, perfectly, slipping over her hips, lying flat over her stomach, the V-neck flattering, the scrunch at one shoulder playing with the light. It was half price.

Sandra got out her Visa card and smiled broadly at the shop assistant.

She was getting better. She was stepping out.

THE man's bathing suit, 1930s, stocking stitch, was in black worsted wool. It was plain knitting for the moment, not very interesting, best done in daylight. The yarn was fine, and it was difficult to pick up dropped stitches unless you could see properly. It was easy work, but tedious because it was easy, and there was a lot of it. Martha had done the shaping around the crotch, and while she knitted black, she eyed the red wool in another basket. It would be much more interesting knitting red, apple red, mailbox red, fire engine red. Martha's hands flew on the needles but her mind darted out and away. Why was she thinking red? Ah, because yesterday she had seen a beautiful red.

Yesterday she had needed to get out. Yesterday, when she had undone the jacket twice, and the wool had started to fray, and the count was wrong for the third time straight, she had zipped up the big bag and gone out.

She had decided on the Botanic Garden for a change of scenery. She would sit in the quiet hush under the Moreton Bay figs and start the black swimsuit.

Lugging her bags along North Terrace, past the hospital where she had visited Cliff, she was nearly to the Garden gate when she saw the red bike.

She clenched her fists in excitement. It had three big

wheels—it was a tricycle! Like the one she had had at the farm when she was small, but this one was enormous, an adult bike, and shiny shiny red, called *crimson* in the paint box. It was speeding along North Terrace and up toward Magill Road, focused and fearless in a dash through an amber light. The handlebars had little white covers on the ends, and there was a hooter, a big hooter. Hoot! Hoot! went the red bike. It made a lot of noise; even buses would be able to hear that hooter. Underneath and behind the two back wheels of the red bike was a basket, a white mesh wire basket full of shopping. Not in plastic bags, but nice cotton bags, and sticking out of the top of one she could see bananas, leafy celery, and a brown head of bread. See, you could go to the market with a bike like that and bring home all your shopping. You could go anywhere. You could go to Alice Springs and back. You could ride away and leave all your mistakes behind.

Martha had seen an adult tricycle before. Barney, who had cerebral palsy, had ridden one around her hometown, but it was a dirty brown, that bike, a man bike. Poor old Barney would lift one hand and stretch the uncooperative muscles of his face into a smile when you waved at him.

But this bike, this modern red bike, was ridden by a young woman, only about thirty, in shorts and a T-shirt, with elegant long legs and a black spiked haircut poking out from under her helmet, and you could see she was happy to be riding that bike along North Terrace. Maybe she put her kids in the basket after school, or maybe she didn't have kids, maybe you wouldn't ever want kids if you had a bike like that.

Red. It was a beautiful colour, that's for sure. Martha kept knitting but stared thoughtfully at the red wool. So much nicer than black. A few stitches into the next row she picked up the red ball of wool and began to knit a pattern into the black, but carefully, on the inside, down low where the man's bottom would be if he put on the bathing suit. It wouldn't have been too comfy when it got wet. The suit would have sagged down with the weight of the water, and stayed wet and cold in the sea breeze, and shrivelled him up to nothing. But when he took it off, he would discover the little bit of red graffiti inside, like a reverse tattoo low on one cheek saying, "Martha was here."

Suddenly the matinee jacket with its problem pattern popped into Martha's mind. It was there, in the nearly full third bag, parked in the corner under the big long zipper that was inclined to stick. She didn't want to think about the jacket. She opened the rubbish chute at the back of her mind, shoved in the matinee jacket thought, and slammed down the lid.

KATE hardly recognised Sandra weaving her way through the pub crowd on Friday night, loaded with shopping bags and wreathed in smiles.

"You look happy! Good day?"

"Excellent!"

"How come?"

"I don't know." Sandra could hardly explain it herself. "Found stuff I wanted, did a base draft for an article, and figured out how to link all the stuff in the exhibition."

"Not bad for Friday!"

"Oh, it's taken all week, of course. But I'm getting somewhere with this knitting thing. It's been great, this little project. Different. And there's quite a lot of interest from the university, which is a bonus. There's so much interest! It seems to have tapped into something in the female academic psyche."

"Because it's not just academic, is it? There's a more basic appeal — the necessity of clothing."

"Maybe. I don't know. Don't care, really." Sandra leaned back and sighed with satisfaction. "It's just been fun, and the interest is a bonus. Just goes to show, you should follow your heart."

"How's Martha doing?"

"Not sure. We had that trip to the mill and she was happy enough then. I've called in a couple of times, but I get leave-me-alone messages. Thought I'd give her some space for a couple of weeks."

They must have been strong messages, thought Kate, for Sandra to notice.

"It's not too pressured for her, is it? That was quite a list."

"No, not for someone like her. You should see her place, Kate! She does this amazing free-form knitting. Wonderful stuff. She must knit all day every day."

Kate shook her head.

"Not possible. Too hard on the body. I ache if I quilt all day, and there's more movement in that than in knitting."

"Perhaps she does some exercise routine to help her manage. She never complains."

"Look after her, Sandra. You'll be struggling if Martha dips out."

"Yes, all right, I'll call in soon." Sandra opened the top of one of her glossy plastic bags.

"Look, Kate, I bought a new dress. First one for two years. Maybe I'll wear it on opening night."

MARTHA looked around her room at the bags of wool, the pattern sheets stuck to the wall, the jam tins bristling with knitting needles, the list of things Sandra had given her to do. Last week it had been exciting; this week it was paralysing. The patterns were difficult, the date was already closer. She would have to knit—how much? She couldn't work it out in her head. She tore open a used envelope and wrote down the number of balls of wool, and the dates, and the list of things to do. If she knitted—she did more calculations—if she knitted eight hours a day, she could do it. And that didn't include pressing or sewing up, or the extra knitting for collars and button bands, and they always took longer than you expected.

But she couldn't settle to work yet, not without a cup of tea. She got down the big mug from the cupboard, the one with the wide top and narrow bottom and the smiling cow with a pendulous udder. She sat on her back step to catch a bit of sun; it was cold in the flat, and the hot cup was warm and comforting in her hands. The potted plants were all dried up, so she took to them with the hose, and then she remembered that they needed fertilising. She went to her little shed and lugged out the fowl manure her brother had brought her from the farm. The lemon tree wasn't doing so well either, so she looked up the gardening book. Well, it must be scale. She would have to go to the nursery for confirmation, but she wouldn't be able to go today because she had all that knitting to do.

The back veranda needed sweeping: dead leaves were havens for nasty crawlies. She swept up and then saw the cobwebs. When that was done, it was a shame to leave the windows so dirty. She wouldn't have enough light to do her knitting properly, and it would comfort her while she was in the house if she could look out and see the birds in the birdbath without being distracted by the streaks of dirt.

If she didn't wash the cloth, it would grow mould and start to smell, so she did that and hung it on the line, and while she was washing that she might as well put her knickers through; with the River Murray in such a terrible state it would be irresponsible to use water just to wash rags.

And so the day went on. When Martha finally sat down to knit, it was four o'clock. She might just squeeze an hour in before it was time to get dinner.

At half past six she heard a knock at the door. Sandra, calling in on her way home from work. Sandra, breezy and cheerful.

"Hi, Martha. Just thought I'd call in and see how you were going."

"OK."

"How much have you done?"

Martha showed her an inch of knitting.

"Not much. Had a bit of trouble with the band. It twisted when I joined it up on the circular needle. So then I had to start again."

"Is this all you've done since last week?"

"No, I've been working on the bathing suit and doing those socks. They take longer than you think. The argyle pattern is slow, and it's only four-ply." She didn't offer to show them to Sandra.

Sandra was disappointed but managed to hold her tongue. She had thought Martha would have at least half of one of the big garments done, at least a back or a front or even a sleeve, but she tried to be generous.

"Never mind. Every job has good days and bad days."

AT HOME, after dinner, Sandra watched the news, but her mind wasn't on it. She finished marking a thesis, but thoughts of Martha nagged away behind her work.

Martha wasn't as organised as Sandra had expected. She'd only knitted bits and pieces, with no appearance of sustained effort. She'd been working for nearly two weeks with little to show for it. Unless she was holding something back. But why would she do that? Martha needed an action plan, a timetable of some kind. If she didn't get her skates on, they wouldn't be ready. Perhaps she'd better call in some other knitters. But then Martha wouldn't get the same attention, and Sandra wanted to give her that, give her the opportunities that would come through public exposure. That wonderful horse!

Another thought nagged at her. Perhaps Martha was knitting other things, like that white business she had taken to the beach house. Perhaps she had other commissions and was keeping them secret.

The exhibition had to go on. She couldn't let Martha jeopardise that. They'd won the funding, the panels had been ordered, the text was well under way. Martha would get her cut of it — an honorarium for the knitting and the profits from any garments sold — and the publicity would ensure further work. There was no grant money left over for the writing. Not that it mattered; it had always been a love job on Sandra's part. Writing the text and collating the oral history fragments were quiet joys. The project had developed its own momentum: Jonty Stewart from New Zealand, unexpected interest from colleagues, a chance meeting with an arts editor, the cache of oral history recordings suddenly available. Even a query from another academic in Canada. She'd call in on Martha in the morning. Martha was the linchpin. She wouldn't be able to get more knitters on such short notice.

The exhibition was the most energizing thing she'd experienced for years. It must not fail. Even as this thought crossed her mind, Sandra sensed a flaw in the glass.

This was what happened when you stayed up too late: you got twitchy and lost your nerve. Get some hot milk, Sandra, and take a sleeping tablet.

MARTHA greeted Sandra cheerfully enough. She'd finished the argyle socks and brought them out to show her. Sandra was affronted by the red, white, and blue.

"I don't remember these colours. A little British, aren't we?"

"I used up some oddments."

"But red, white, and blue?"

"They go well together, and that's what the pattern said. Anyway, who said they're British? They could be Australian—or American. Would you rather have stars and stripes? Not a problem."

Sandra glanced at her. Was Martha capable of those kinds of ironies?

"Do you think you can get it done? It's a lot of work."

"I always do what I'm asked," said Martha stiffly. "You can count on me."

"I thought perhaps we could make some kind of timetable. You know, all the parts that need to be knitted, and some dates. So you can pace yourself."

"I won't let you down, I promise."

"Look, how about this?" Sandra had ruled up a progress grid for each of the garments. "See, you can do them one at a time, or several at once if you want variety. Then you won't get bored."

Martha could see that Sandra didn't have any idea. She hadn't allowed for sewing up, or for the embroidery on the bed jacket. She had assumed that the baby's jacket would take half as long as the adult jumper, simply because it was smaller, not realising that because it was finer and in five pieces, it would take at least the same amount of time.

"Thanks, Sandra. I can work it out myself."

"You could draw up your own version if this doesn't suit."

"I'll think about it."

As she knitted through the afternoon, to some difficult music on Radio National, Martha wondered why she hadn't been honest. She felt guilty, that's why, because she had mucked around all day yesterday.

It wasn't Sandra's fault; she just didn't know how much work it was. And it wasn't all that much, really: a dress, a skirt, a couple of jumpers, a few socks, a vest, the straps for the man's bathing suit, and the "war comforts." Comforts. There wasn't much comfort in them.

She knitted all day, had a quick dinner, and knitted into the night. When she went to bed she had pins and needles in her fingers, and her back and neck ached. Crazy, deadset crazy. She should never have said yes.

SANDRA couldn't sleep, but for once it wasn't sadness that kept her awake. It was sheer excitement, the old research juices flowing, the lure of the library and the Internet. Already she had filled half a drawer of the filing cabinet. She hadn't anticipated that there would be so much contemporary knitting. The trend might have started as a marketing ploy by the wool industry, but it had certainly taken off; that kind of thing was successful only if people were ready for it. The new yoga, they called it, the new community: the peaceful clacking of needles creating a heartbeat, a rhythm of rest, a meditative oasis in the midst of a frantic lifestyle. A whole new range of fabrics was being created from an amazing variety of exotic textures and colours. The knitting itself was simple, even Sandra could see that, but the choice of yarns was mind-boggling.

In the beginning the exhibition was for garments from 1900 to 2000. But the new wave of interest in the last few years certainly deserved attention.

"I'M TIRED," Martha said to Cliff. "I'm so tired. I'm not sleeping. At night the patterns go round and round in my head, but I never get to cast off and put the needles back in the cupboard. I never get to lie down and think that tomorrow will be a rest day, because I can't rest now, I don't know how. I used to just go and look at the universe wall and think about the stars and the sun and how fantastic it is that we're all part of that dance, but now it just doesn't work. I feel like I'm in prison. I've lost the song." She rubbed the back of her hand on the side of her nose.

For once Cliff didn't know what to say. He worked his mouth, trying to see if it would shape some words, but none came. He wanted to give her a hug, but he didn't know if that was allowed. A while back she had slapped at him and told him to keep his hands to himself.

"Do you want a cup of tea?" he said.

Martha didn't answer. She kept knitting, fast, her head down. She was like a soldier, shooting stitches with her needles. Cliff winced.

"Why don't you have a rest?" he said.

Martha jabbed a look at him.

"I can't. The exhibition opens in fourteen weeks, and

I've got to finish this jacket, make a skirt, a sleeping suit, another jumper, and do the things from both world wars. Oh, and there's a baby's layette to finish. I'll never get it all done."

Cliff was watching her ball of wool, twisting and turning on the floor like a mad little mouse.

It jerked toward his chair. Cliff put his foot on it.

Martha didn't notice until she used up the slack.

"Now what!" She pulled it hard, but Cliff's foot didn't budge.

"Get off it, you big lummox."

"Do you want a cup of tea?"

"Get off my wool!"

Cliff folded his arms and left his foot where it was. "You need a break, my girl."

"Shut up, Cliff. Get your big fat foot off my wool."

Martha was scaring him, but he didn't budge. "You should tell Sandra where to stick it. The world won't fall in if you don't finish it all."

"Yes it will. Sandra's already done all the wall labels to go with the work. There'll be holes and empty places if I don't do it."

"This is supposed to be a hobby. Fun."

"Well, it's not. It's work."

"Are you getting any money for it?"

"I don't know. Give me my wool."

"Mattie! Haven't you asked her?"

"I could probably sell some stuff."

"Do you mean you're doing it for nothing?"

"I was doing it for love."

Cliff snorted.

"What's she getting out of it?"

Martha shrugged. "I don't know. We just thought it would be interesting to do, that's all. Because we like the old stuff, from the war and all that. She's not getting anything out of it."

"She writes things. I bet she's written about you, and all those bigwigs are reading it."

Martha stood up, stepped on Cliff's toe, hard, and retrieved her wool.

"Bigwigs wouldn't be interested in knitting."

"Don't you bet on it," said Cliff. "They get paid for it. They think people like us are insects. They study us."

"What are you, then? A cockroach?"

Martha was knitting fast again, her face set in hard lines.

"And you're Miss Busy Bitch. I mean Bee! Miss Busy Bee!"

Martha glared at him, packed up her knitting, and said, "Go home. I'm going to bed."

"Oh, come on, Mattie, have a cuppa with me first."

"No. Out, cockroach. Go home."

THE phone rang and Sandra jumped. When she answered, there was no response. She hung up again. It was unnerv-

ing, getting called and nobody answering. Made you wonder if someone was thinking of breaking in and just checking to see if you were home.

When it rang a second time, there was another
silence, but this time it was followed by the click-click
of falling coins.

"Hello?"

"Hello, Sandra, guess who?" said a voice. Sandra
recoiled at the unfamiliar voice using her first name.

"If you don't tell me, I'll hang up," she said.

"Don't get your knickers in a knot," said the voice.
"It's me, Cliff. You know, Martha's mate."

Ah. Sandra had an image of stubble, missing teeth,
odd socks.

"Oh, Cliff!" She tried to keep the relief out of her
voice. "What can I do for you?"

"I'm worried about Martha. She's working too hard."

"What do you mean?"

"All that knitting. She's not coping."

"Well, it's kind of you to be concerned, Cliff, but
Martha's an adult. I'm sure she'd tell me if she wasn't managing."

"No," said Cliff. "That's just it. She wouldn't. She
won't take any time off."

Ah, thought Sandra, poor old boy's feeling neglected.

"Well, thanks for telling me, Cliff. I'll keep it in
mind."

She hung up and sighed. Only Cliff. Wouldn't hurt a

fly, Martha had said. Nothing to be jumpy about. But he should mind his own business all the same.

MARTHA was ashamed. Cliff was trying to be kind, she knew. And why was she working like a mad thing? There was no joy in it anymore. There was no anticipation, no mulling over the pattern, feeling the way toward a new gift, a new recipient. Watching someone, trying to work out what they would like.

What would happen if she just stopped? What would happen if she died tomorrow, fell down dead? What would Sandra do then?

She, Martha, had made a mistake, that's what. A big mistake. She'd said yes instead of no, and now she was in a tangle. And when she got into a tangle, it took years to get out of it. Like those other times, those times when she had done all those other things she didn't want to do, saying yes when she really wanted to say no. All her gates were broken. People just went in and out as they pleased, and she just let them.

She'd made a big mistake, and she didn't know how to undo it. Sandra needed her, and Sandra was her friend, and she couldn't let her down.

Yes, Sandra, she'd said. But now she, Martha, had started to unravel. Soon there would be nothing left.

FEBRUARY

OUTSIDE IT WAS like a furnace. Televisions everywhere blared bushfire warnings. Cliff bought himself a scratchie and a milkshake and found himself a cool corner in the food hall, where he sat down with the bright new cardboard and got out his lucky coin. Scratch scratch. Only two squares left, one each side of the feather. It wasn't looking good, but you could never tell, you could never tell. He started at the bottom corner of the fifth square, and then there it was, the edge of a—heart! Two hearts. He turned the ticket upside down and started in the middle of the last square, gently, so as not to damage the image. It was dark in the middle, and it looked like a—no? Was it? Yes! YES! It was a third heart. Three hearts! Three happy hilarious hearts and two thousand bloody beautiful buckaroos. Three hearts full of happiness and hope. Three whole hearts lucky for love.

Cliff sat at the plastic table. The cleaner came and took away his empties and wiped down the table, and still he sat with the scratchie in his hand, beaming at the freshly cleaned table. His body was motionless, but in his head he was down in Gawler Place, he was walking around the corner, he was not standing outside the glass window as he had a hundred times; this time he was pushing open the swing door and walking past all the brightly lit silver machines, right up to the counter, and he was slapping down two thousand dollars in hundred-dollar notes and buying Martha the best bloody knitting machine they had in the shop.

SANDRA was at home, writing. It had taken her three hours to write two hundred words. To give her body a break she had gone outside into the bright heat of the garden and pulled up some weeds in the shade of the walnut tree. Her hands busy, her mind still pushed and shoved at words as she tried to pare down the text she was writing for the exhibition to lean muscle, to get each muscly word working with the next one, so the meaning pumped through the whole from beginning to end. When she returned to the house, shuttered against the heat, she was momentarily blinded by the dark.

She sat down at her desk and rewrote the passage, then read it again. Did the words say what she wanted them to say? Would a reader take away what she had spent so much time putting in?

It doesn't matter, she told herself. You can't control

the interpretation. Let it go. And suddenly she thought of Martha's orange horse, standing there with its ears cocked forward, listening intently to the silence. What was it Martha wanted to say with that horse? Just a bit of fun, she had said. But it had to be more than that.

Soon after visiting Martha that first time, Sandra had shown her an article about Bronwen Sandland, a visual artist who had knitted a housecosy for her house. Martha read it with interest but was not particularly impressed.

"Waste of wool," she said.

"What about your horse, then?" asked Sandra.

"Someone gave me that yarn," said Martha. "And it's not wool, it's acrylic. You wouldn't want to wear it. A horse is all it's good for."

"Lots of people wear acrylic."

"Not me," said Martha firmly. "It doesn't breathe properly. And I don't knit it either."

"You knitted the horse."

"Yes, well, someone who didn't know better was trying to be kind. So I took it."

"But what if you were allergic to wool?"

"There's other natural fibres," said Martha. "But wool is best, it's soft and wears well. There was a dead sheep once, and the fleece was out in the paddock for fifty years, and a British wool firm made a suit out of it." She was watching Sandra closely, and there was something in Martha's eyes that Sandra hadn't seen before.

"But if you can't stand wool, there's plenty of choice —silk, cotton, linen, llama, alpaca, angora, rabbit, even undercoat from dogs. Made a great pair of mittens once from a golden retriever. Fantastic colour, and soft. Shall I make you a pair?"

Was Martha sending her up? Sandra took the question at face value, declined the offer as politely as she could and quickly went home.

MARTHA was startled by a sharp rap at the front door. When she opened it, a man in some kind of uniform, with a logo on the chest of his green jumper, stood before her. She didn't recognise the logo.

"Martha McKenzie?" he asked.

"Yes."

"Special delivery. Just sign here and I'll bring it in."

"What am I signing?" Martha knew about signing and fine print and that you had to be careful.

"It's just to say that you've received this delivery."

"What delivery?"

"I don't know, madam. My job is just to bring it, not to know what it is."

Martha was mystified.

"But I didn't order anything. Are you sure there's not a mistake?"

He checked the paperwork. No, he assured her, there was no mistake.

Martha wouldn't sign until she had seen the boxes and the address labels. She held the door open while the man brought them in, one at a time, obviously heavy. He left them, piled up, a flat brown castle in the middle of her living room.

Martha shut her front door and sat down to stare at them. They didn't move.

Ten minutes later she fetched her large scissors, cut the heavy sticky tape, and carefully opened the thick brown paper. Underneath were two plain brown cardboard boxes. On the end of one she saw the word KNITTING.

Knitting machine, that's what it was. A knitting machine.

Martha had just started reading the manual when there was another knock at the door. It was Cliff, with a bunch of marigolds.

"What's this?" he said, looking surprised.

Martha told him.

"Where did that come from?"

"I don't know. I'm going to ring up and find out." Cliff held his breath while Martha made the call. She came back frowning.

"I rang up the place it came from, and they said someone paid cash and told them to send it here. A gift, they said."

"Do lessons come with it?"

"I didn't ask. But I can work it out myself.

A neighbour near the farm had one, though not as flash as this. It's the same brand."

For the next couple of hours Cliff helped Martha, flattening the packaging, taking it out to the bin, screwing bits together, holding and helping.

Martha was in a flap. "I don't know about this. It would be so quick. You can knit a jumper in a day with this thing. But the stuff I'm doing for Sandra is supposed to be hand-knitting. No one had these machines in the old days."

"But you do it with your hands, so it's still hand-knitting."

"Yes, but it's not genuine, is it?"

WHEN Sandra saw the knitting machine, she didn't know what to think. Martha saw straightaway that whoever her benefactor might be, it certainly wasn't Sandra.

"You mean it just showed up?"

"Yep. In the mailbox."

Sandra raised her eyebrows.

"Not really in the mailbox. But like a letter. Out of the blue."

"Any idea who sent it?"

"Nope."

Sandra went through her own mental checklist. Kate had told her of such gifts in the context of her church, but surely no one there knew Martha well enough. Kate and

Tony? No. Sandra knew that money was tight with Tony's new business.

"What does the fabric look like?" asked Sandra.

"Well, like this. Like hand-knitting, but finer and smoother." Martha showed Sandra a piece the size of a cushion cover. Sandra examined it.

"How quick is it?"

Martha smiled and slid a silver mechanism along the needles.

"That's a row."

"What about the shaping, and the colours?"

"I've been looking at the book. If we did everything in five-ply it would be OK. But it wouldn't be the genuine article. Would it?"

"But it would be much quicker?"

"Oh, yes."

"Well, how about you make one thing, and then we'll talk about it?"

"It won't be authentic hand-knitting."

"It's handmade, though," said Sandra. "I know that boutiques sell clothing made by women with knitting machines, and it's still called handmade."

"But it's not hand-knitting," said Martha.

"Close enough. It will still show what the clothes were really like. You can sew them up roughly if you think they need to look more homespun. No, no, I didn't mean it, Martha. I know you take pride in your work. And anyway, Martha, knitting machines are part of the history of knitting. The first one was invented in the fifteen hundreds, to make stockings. They called it frame-knitting. So you shouldn't really object. And I don't think we've got a choice, have we? You're so far behind now—unless we do it this way it will never get done."

Martha's face had the blank look that Sandra remembered from her years of secondary school teaching. It was the kind of face you got when you had put a kid totally offside.

MARTHA had a quick dinner and decided to try something more complex than a cushion cover. The pattern book had a man's sleeveless vest similar to the one in the war book, a bold Fair Isle. The instructions were clear, the machine worked like a dream; she finished the vest and sewed it up before midnight. So easy-peasy.

She called Sandra the following morning as she had arranged. "I've finished the vest."

"Already!"

"Yes, but you can't have it."

"Can I come and see it?"

"All right. But it's not going to work."

Sandra came over straightaway.

"Looks all right to me."

"But it's not. It's not the real thing. I couldn't sleep for thinking about it."

"But Martha, it's the reproduction that's important, not how it's reproduced. People can see what the clothes were like. Most people won't even know."

"Any knitter would. Even you would know, and you don't knit."

"But Martha, don't you see, it doesn't really matter. The kind of knitting doesn't matter. A knitting machine is part of the history of knitting. Using a machine to help create replicas—it's all one and the same."

"Not to me. There are plenty of machine-knitters out there. Get someone else to do it."

"But I want you! Don't you want to show off your skill? Show what you can do? This is your exhibition."

Martha gave her a look that was hard to interpret.

"I'll hand-knit for you, but I'm not putting my name to this stuff. It's not right to pretend they're hand knits when they're not."

"Don't be such a purist, Martha! This is a technological age. Besides, I'm the one with the responsibility. We're a bit behind, and this is a great way to catch up. If you don't deliver, I'm the one who'll have to explain. You don't want to let me down, do you?" Sandra didn't like what she heard coming out of her own mouth. Emotional blackmail. But she had to galvanise Martha somehow.

"I can't get it done if you stand here yabbering all

day," said Martha. "Go on, Sandra, go to work, so I can too."

WHEN Cliff came by a couple of hours later, the knitting machine, packed back in its boxes, was sitting on the front doorstep. Martha was sitting on the doorstep too, knitting fast.

"What are you doing out here?" asked Cliff.

"Waiting."

"What for?"

"The Salvation Army truck. I'm giving the machine to them."

"How come? I thought it was just what you wanted. And you need it."

"Nope. Don't like it. Don't want it. It's all right for other people, but it's not right for me."

"But it would save so much time!"

"Shut up, Cliff, you sound just like Sandra. I'm not having it. That's that."

Cliff sat next to her on the step, watching Martha's busy fingers.

Two thousand beautiful buckaroos.

"What about the person who gave it to you?" asked Cliff.

"I don't know where it's from. They never asked me if I wanted it. It was just anonymous, so I can't give it back."

Cliff stared ahead without seeing anything.

"Was it too hard to use?" he said at last.

"Oh, I can use it all right. There's a vest in there you can have, hanging on the back of the chair, that I made on that machine. Take it away before Sandra gets her hands on it. But I just don't want to use that thing. I'm not that kind of knitter. Besides, the Salvos will find good use for it."

Cliff went in and tried on the vest, which fitted him perfectly. He paraded before her and tried to persuade her to keep the machine. He was risking fury, he could see. Martha would not budge.

Perhaps he should try and get his money back. But he didn't want her to know who gave it to her. Especially now that she so clearly didn't want it.

"Shall I take it away for you?"

Martha laughed. "Thanks, but it's too heavy for you, mate. And the Salvos will be here any minute."

And there came the truck down the street. Cliff watched the Salvo men carry his prize away. It was now or never. He had to make up his mind. As the driver turned on the engine, Cliff tapped on the window. The driver wound it down and looked at him quizzically.

"*Influence is not government*," said Cliff. "George Washington," he offered by way of explanation. The driver stared at him.

"It's a bloody expensive machine, mate. Make sure it gets a good home."

The driver saluted and drove off.

And it was a bloody expensive vest he was wearing, that was for sure.

But by the time Cliff walked back to his cubby half an hour later, he was reconciled to the idea. Plenty of winter nights he'd stayed at the Salvos' emergency accommodation. Next time he needed a bed, he wouldn't feel so guilty. And there was always the next scratchie, the next horse. It wasn't really a big deal.

SANDRA was knitting a scarf in Martha's tiny living room. At work earlier that day she had decided to try to bridge the increasing sense of distance between herself and Martha. Maybe they could have a companionable time together. She brought coffee and chocolate, a peace offering. She would be humble and spend time under Martha's tuition. The scarf was simple, even rows of stripes, nothing fancy. It might do as a war-effort piece.

Sitting opposite, Martha was knitting long skinny triangular pieces for a skirt. Sandra was hoping that she would get out the pieces she had already done and lay them on the floor, as she had a couple of weeks earlier with a 1910 dress. Sandra wanted to see the whole. Sandra always wanted to see the whole thing, the big pattern, the long chain of cause and effect. History spread out. If you understood the past, you might be able to prepare for the future.

They had knitted for over an hour with barely ten words between them. It was hard to know what to talk about. Sandra made another attempt.

"When did you start that skirt?"

"Two days ago."

"What pattern are you doing?"

"Just stocking stitch."

"Don't you ever get tired of knitting?"

"Sometimes."

It was hopeless. Martha was shut down, incommunicado. Sandra had decided to pack up and go home, when she noticed a mistake in her work. She had dropped a dark purple stitch, hard to see in the artificial light, and it had run down four rows below. She held the knitting closer to her glasses and angled her elbow to pick it up.

"What's the matter?" asked Martha.

"Dropped a stitch."

Sandra worked on in silence. Martha, knitting steadily, watched her.

Sandra sighed. "I can't get it. The more I work on it, the further down it goes. I'll have to undo it all."

"Give it to me."

Like a child, Sandra handed over her knitting. Martha turned the work so that it caught the light.

"You're lucky. It's fixable." She took a crochet hook from the table beside her. Sandra watched as Martha's thick fingers deftly caught the dropped stitch, knitted it up through the missed rows, popped it back on the needle and handed it back.

"Your tension is good now; it's about the same as mine. You could do some of this skirt if you wanted to. Do you want to knit a panel?"

"I don't really have time."

"You're here now."

"Tonight's my only night free this week."

"What about your lunch break? Couldn't you do it then?"

"No." Sandra had visions of herself sitting in the history staff room, knitting her scarf or a bit of Martha's skirt. Being questioned about it by the eminent visiting historian, from whom she was hoping to extract an introduction to a university in Germany. Justifying the pattern as a genuine 1932 reproduction. Being smiled at, condescendingly. The funny little knitting woman.

"Why not?"

"You just don't do that sort of thing at my work."

"How come?"

"I don't know. You just don't. It's not appropriate. It would be like knitting at a funeral."

"But I thought you said you were interested in women's work. The history and the culture and that."

"Yes, I am, but that doesn't mean I actually do it. Not seriously, anyway. That's for specialists like you." The words slipped easily from her tongue. "When you think about it, and talk about it and write about it, it's more about"—Sandra struggled to say it simply—"the idea of women's work."

"It's not much use then, is it?"

"What do you mean?"

"Well, you said this exhibition was a 'feminist celebration of domesticity.' " Martha, quoting from the invitation, fresh from the printer, rolled her eyes as she said it. "But if you don't actually *do* domestic stuff, if you don't believe in it enough to do it yourself, it's not much use, is it? It's just words in your head, and meanwhile your back gets cold."

"Don't knock words," said Sandra. "They're the best form of communication we've got. Besides, I am doing it. I'm sitting right here with you, doing it."

"Not really," said Martha. "You're knitting something for yourself, not for the exhibition. And you don't enjoy it. You just want to keep an eye on me."

Sandra was stung. Martha was watching her, beadily, still knitting fast.

"Yes, I wanted to see you working. I like watching you. And I am worried you won't finish in time, so I guess you're right in a way. But it's more than that, Martha. I enjoy your company. And I want to do something different, get better at knitting. It's good to try to do something with my hands, even if I'm not good at it. But you didn't really want me here tonight. I'm sorry for being in the way." There was a genuine humility in her voice.

That night in the bathroom, systematically cleaning

her teeth, Martha looked in the mirror and saw that her reflection was hard and angry, with tears in its eyes. She was unravelling, and knitting herself into something else, something ugly, something miserable and nasty, something worse than a mistake.

MARCH

MARTHA WAS NOT sleeping well. She kept waking up sweating, even with her little fan turned directly at the bed. She'd doze off, then suddenly jerk awake. Sandra's list of requirements ran around inside her head like a nest of angry ants. When she finally slept, her work still tumbled about in her head. Patterns, numbers, needles. She was caught up in wool, winding around her softly and surely as cobweb. And here was Sandra coming toward her, hefting something almighty heavy, using both hands.

Martha couldn't make out what Sandra was dragging behind her. Then she saw that it was her own three bags, her three bags full of mistakes, the big stripy bag, the carpetbag, and the heavy brown suitcase. Sandra's face was as stern as a law court. She stopped in front of Martha and opened the stripy bag and pulled out the first garment, the baby's matinee jacket with the scalloped edge that had gone wrong in the middle of the left front. And then a little top she had been making for her niece, and after that another piece of big green knitting, and so they kept coming, all the errors Martha had ever made, starting with the matinee jacket, working back through the forty-plus years of her long knitting life. The unfinished hat for her cousin, the gloves with the holes where the fingers joined on, the puckered waist of a child's dress, even a hot water bottle cover she had once started making for Manny. So many wrong things, more than Martha could count, more than she knew she had, a great pile growing and growing from the bottomless bag. Sandra and Martha were stepping and clambering over them like too much washing on the laundry floor. Martha tried to stop Sandra, tried to stuff everything back where it belonged, but Sandra laughed and skipped away to the top of another pile of rejects, where she hauled up the carpetbag and unclasped it with small, strong fingers. A great clump of knitting burst out, the yellowed cotton tablecloth Martha had started for Malcolm's wife and in her anger had never finished, a series of ugly potholders for a charity stall, a tea cosy with no hole for the spout. No matter how many things Sandra pulled from the bags, there was always something more, another error of judgement, another bad feeling, everything bristling with needles and tape measures, stitch holders and thousands of wool ends never darned in, tangled knitting and crumpled bits of difficult pattern, scrappy bits of paper covered in Martha's frantic writing trying to get the things right. Such a waste of wool and time and effort, such a waste, all her nastiness and inadequacy piled up for every-one to see. The unbearable shame of it, and nowhere to hide.

No! Martha shouted out. No! No! Stop! But her voice was tiny and ineffectual, with no power against San-dra, who kept on, relentless and merciless, flicking open the rusty metal latches on the old brown suitcase that Martha hadn't opened for years, dragging out dingy brown garments from a time in hospital, misshapen teenage attempts at clinging mohair cardigans, dirty little bits of knitting from childhood. And now Sandra was jeer-ing and prancing about on it. Martha could hear the pat-terns tearing and the needles snapping as Sandra held up Martha's miserable life, item by item, all the things that Martha had made to cover herself, to hide and please and pacify.

It was hot. Martha was sweating, boiling with embar-rassment, her face and hands slick with perspiration as she chased Sandra through piles of garments that reached up to tangle around her legs. Sandra, light as a feather, danced away, mean and accusing, and out of reach.

Martha gave a great cry of pain and shame and fury, and woke herself up.

She switched on the light. Around her everything was neat and orderly, her clothes folded on the chair, her slip-pers cheek to cheek like an old married couple, her glasses and watch side by side on the bedside table. All just as it should be, except the bed, which was a mess. The sheets were damp, her nightie was drenched. She could feel perspiration running sideways from her forehead to her pillow. She ached all over.

She was sick, that was it. She was sick and she'd had a nightmare, just a nightmare, not real. Sandra wasn't really like that, she wasn't like that at all. But the bags and their contents were real, that was the trouble. Martha's face flamed at the thought of them.

The pain started then, vague at first, low in her belly and around in her back, a dragging feverish pain that wouldn't localise and wouldn't go away.

For the rest of that troubled night Martha rocked with the pain. It didn't occur to her that she could get help, that she could ring a doctor for advice or call an ambulance. She knew Mary Sherbet next door would jump at a chance to do something for her, but she didn't have the energy to cope with Mary Sherbet fussing around in her pink pompom slippers. It never crossed her mind to let Sandra know that she was ill or to ring her brother, far away on the farm. Martha did what she always did in the face of bad trouble: she retreated deep down inside herself, where it was dark and warm, and waited till things improved up on the surface.

She took a couple of painkillers, fished out from a pocket in a knitting bag, and though they soothed her a little, she began to alternate between heat and shivering. In the middle of the night she refilled her hot water bottle and got the old baby blanket out of the camphor chest. She remade the bed, smoothed the sheets she had rucked with her tossing, and gave her pillow a couple of feeble bangs against the wall. Tucking herself back under the quilt, she shut her eyes and held a corner of the camphor-fragrant blanket close to her nose.

The pain went on and on. She made it into shapes. Her guts were winding up like a ball of wool. A pair of knitting needles was stabbing at her soft insides. Scissors were going snippety snip at the back of her rib cage. Maybe she had rocks in her belly. She drew her knees up and lay face down in the pillow, leaning on her elbows, rocking to and fro. Was this what it was like having a baby? She got colder and colder, until her teeth rattled in her head like a tin box full of marbles. She was so hot she threw off all the blankets and lay sweating on the sheet.

But behind the pain and confusion and semi-madness was something else, a sensation just beyond her nerve ends, a kind of singing. The singing carried on, regardless of the heat and cold, deeper than the chills and the furnace, never loud or even insistent, simply there. It was a high, thin music pulling at the edge of consciousness, toothache sweet, a counterpoint melody to pain. Through the throbbing drumbeat of Martha's misery it transposed itself, time and time again, in a thousand different variations.

SANDRA looked at her watch and apologised to Kate.

"Sorry, I'd better go, it's getting late. I just want to pass by Martha's. We didn't part well last time, and I need to touch base. If her light's off I won't go in."

Sandra wasn't sure about Martha's sleeping habits, though she suspected Martha was an early riser. It was after ten, but the light was still on. Sandra knocked.

Martha opened the door and Sandra took a step backward. Martha looked like a refugee from a war zone. Her hair was loose and stringy, she was wearing a dirty cardigan over a nightie, there were hollow shadows under her eyes.

"Martha! Are you all right?"

"No. Excuse me." Martha disappeared, leaving Sandra on the doorstep. Sandra stepped inside the door and heard retching from the bathroom.

"Can I come in?"

There was no reply. Sandra waited. Martha came back, steadying herself against the wall, almost falling into a chair.

"How long have you been sick?"

"Don't know. Three days, maybe."

"Have you seen a doctor?"

"No."

"How long have you been vomiting?"

Martha tried to think. "Don't know."

"Come on, I'm taking you to the hospital." Martha stayed miserably hunched in the chair while Sandra got her slippers and a coat, but at the last minute Martha said feebly, "I need my bags."

"No you don't," said Sandra. "You're sick. I've packed everything you need. Come on."

"I've got to have them."

"What for? What's in them?"

"Things I need."

"Look, Martha," said Sandra gently, kneeling down next to her, "you're sick. Whatever is in them will just have to wait. Come on."

"Not going without them."

Martha's cheeks were pink with fever, her eyes glittered with determined tears. Sandra sighed.

"Oh, all right. Come on, then. But one will do, surely." The carpetbag, the smallest.

"No. I need them all." Martha was distressed and sick. Sandra didn't have the heart to persist.

By the time she got Martha to the emergency room at the big city hospital, it was after eleven-thirty. There were only fifteen-minute parking spaces available. Sandra, carrying Martha's bags, walked her in to the bright lights of Casualty and found her a seat. There was a line at the desk; she'd better find a park and help Martha with the paperwork later.

Eventually she found a vacant parking space at the back of the hospital. Taking what she thought was a shortcut on her way back, she became disoriented and found herself at the junction of two long corridors. Which way? At one end she saw a man dressed in white and pushing a soft wide broom.

"Lost?" he asked kindly as she hurried toward him.

"Yes. Where's Casualty?"

"Come with me. I'll show you the way."

There were many twists and turns, more than Sandra would have thought possible. She glanced at her companion. He had a stillness about him that was comforting.

"How do you ever find your way about?" she asked.

"Oh, I've been here a long time," he said. "Cleaner, guide, visitor—whatever. Here we are."

And there was Martha, still seated with her head against the pillar. Sandra turned to thank the man, but he had gone.

After the quiet, cool walk through the hospital, Sandra suddenly felt she was entering some kind of surreal comedy. Martha hadn't moved since Sandra had left her. People waited everywhere, propped on chairs, parked on beds, listlessly watching the TV blaring from a screen too high for anyone to see comfortably. Young interns in white coats looked tired and harried. Posters on the walls showed detailed pictures of the digestive system, melanomas, lung disease. Sandra's heart sank. Oh, yes. Public hospitals. She suddenly remembered the rumours of long waits, though with her private health insurance she had not taken much notice.

Martha was still wearing her overcoat and shivering, though the night was warm. Earlier, in the car, reaching for the hand brake, Sandra had brushed against Martha's hand and felt the heat coiling off her, dry heat, like a hot Adelaide summer. But still Martha shivered, thrusting her hands deep in her pockets. It was obvious that she wanted to lie down. Only the straight, hard back of the waiting-room chair kept her upright.

Sandra spoke briefly to her and went to the desk with Martha's Medicare card to fill out the forms. She had not been inside a hospital since Jack died; everything in her wanted to retreat. She hoped that when the staff saw how sick Martha was they'd rush her through. Sandra had an early start the next day, with back-to-back commitments both morning and afternoon. She couldn't afford to be here too long.

"How long will we have to wait?" she asked the woman behind the counter.

"Depends. You'll be seen in order of priority, not arrival. We get accidents."

"She's very feverish."

"Yes, I can see she's miserable. We'll do our best."

Sandra watched the woman checking the forms. She had a kind face, but she looked tired. The graveyard shift. She looked up, her finger halfway down the page.

"Are you next of kin?"

"No. Why?"

"We need her next of kin. Are you a relative? Partner?"

Sandra snorted a surprised laugh. "No. Just a friend."

"Well, we need all the details. Could you ask her, please?"

Sandra went back to Martha.

"You have to put next of kin on the form. What shall I write?"

"Mal."

"Mal?"

"My brother, the one that helped me buy the flat. The farmer." Martha gave the address and phone number. Sandra wrote the phone number down for herself as well, handed the form back, and went to sit by Martha. It was going to be a long wait. She picked up a magazine.

"JACQUI TEMPLE'S SECRET ABORTION" shouted a headline. Who was Jacqui Temple? Sandra kept on reading; Martha glanced at the article in Sandra's lap and turned her head away. Sandra flicked through the pages. What did she know about Martha, really? Only what Martha chose to tell. Was she more fragile than she looked, as Kate had suggested? Was Martha's version of herself true? Sandra had never bothered to probe further. It took energy to ask, to get to know someone, and Sandra had been too full of her work, too full of her own survival, to think about Martha.

"I'm going to throw up."

Sandra looked around. She was no good at this. What

did you do with an adult who wanted to vomit in a public place and who wasn't well enough to make it to the toilet? The two potted plants looked totally inadequate. She approached the reception desk and stood in front of the same woman.

"My friend is nauseous."

The woman glanced at Martha.

"Come in here."

Sandra picked up the bags, and the nurse led them into a bay where half a dozen people were lying on beds. A student nurse half pulled the curtain around them, but the end was left open, and the old man opposite, with his plump little wife, stared straight back. The nurse handed Martha a stainless steel bowl, into which she promptly vomited. The nurse took it away and brought it back clean. Or was it a new one? Martha was holding a hanky to her mouth with her eyes screwed up.

Sandra fought a rising agitation. Hospital memories jabbed. She didn't want to be here: it was too soon. They had had their share of emergency admissions. Jack, too, had vomited, his skin yellow with jaundice; near the end, even the sheets had yellow smudges. She could hardly stand it.

Get a grip on yourself, Sandra. She turned back to Martha, who retched again. Sandra turned her face away: it seemed rude to look at someone in such an intimate moment. The spasm passed.

"Are you in pain?"

Martha nodded and pointed to her back.

"Here. It's quite bad, really. But I've stopped feeling sick." Her breathing was short and shallow, and her face was damp and shiny now. She had thrown off her jacket. She handed the bowl to Sandra, who stood holding it helplessly, then put it on the stainless steel trolley next to a pile of sealed syringes.

"Do you want me to rub your back?"

Martha shook her head vehemently.

They would just have to wait.

Martha was cold. Sandra took off her jacket and threw it over the hospital blanket for extra warmth.

After an hour Sandra went back to the desk.

"Just how long is this going to take?"

"I'm sorry. It's order of priority. We've had a gunshot wound and a cardiac arrest."

"My friend is really sick. This just isn't good enough. One minute she's hot and then she gets the chills."

"I'm sorry. We can't do anything about it until she sees the registrar. If you want to be seen more quickly you'll have to go to a private twenty-four-hour clinic."

Sandra went back to Martha and offered to take her somewhere else. She, Sandra, would be happy to pay. Martha wouldn't go.

"No, here now. Don't want to move. You go home."

Sandra thought about the lecture she was to give in

the morning. And then two meetings and a double tutorial. She could feel herself getting more and more agitated. She had to get out.

"It's just that I have to work tomorrow."

"I know. Kind of you to bring me. I'll be fine."

Just then a nurse came in.

"I'll take your temperature." She pressed the thermometer into Martha's ear.

"You're a regular little tropical paradise." She swept Sandra's jacket away. "Who put this on you?"

"I did. She was cold."

"I know you feel cold," said the nurse to Martha, ignoring Sandra, but speaking for her benefit nonetheless. "But that's because you've got a temperature. Your body is trying to cool you down. You mustn't rug up, it will make you worse. Leave it off."

Martha's teeth were chattering. She looked utterly miserable. For a second Sandra saw Jack's face superimposed on Martha's. She reached out a hand instinctively and placed it on Martha's arm. Martha still radiated heat like an oven.

"Are you really sure you don't need me?"

"No. Go."

Sandra left the cubicle where Martha lay in a shivering huddle on the bed. She gave her name and phone number to the woman at the counter and headed for the exit. She wanted to run. The big double doors slid open.

A cold front had come through, and the night air slapped at her face. The car, covered in dew, was bleak and cold. Her panic began to subside. She wiped the back window with her bare hand.

It didn't feel good enough, leaving Martha there like that, all by herself. But it's not life-threatening, she told herself. She's just got an infection or something. She's safe there, in good hands. What can happen? And they've got the phone number. Martha's managed all her life by herself. Give yourself a break.

Back in bed, the electric blanket on high to warm her cold body, Sandra couldn't sleep. Too busy justifying abandoning Martha. She tried the rational approach.

Come on, she told herself, you've got students dependent on you. You took the initiative, you took her to hospital. What more do you want?

But the accusing finger still wagged. Traitor. She knew what it was, of course. She could see it now, Jack's white cheekbone turned away from her, toward the window and the light.

"Leave me," he had said. "Go and get some rest."

She had gone. And when she came back, he had gone.

THE following day, when Sandra went to the hospital, she could hear Martha's voice, loud and monotonous, even before she reached the room. The curtain was drawn around the bed. Sandra stood still and listened.

"My name is Martha, make no mistake," it said. "I don't like mistakes. I don't like mistakes in knitting. I like knitting but not making knitting mistakes. I like order. I like the order knitting makes. If you knit one, purl one, repeat, all along the row, and back again the same, you make rib. That's on even stitches. If you have odd stitches you make moss stitch. Rib is for ribbing, for cuffs and collars and bands on the bottom, for necklines, and puckers in patterns. Puckers, evenly spaced, drawn in and stretching out, make for interest. I'm interested in knitting. I'm very interested in knitting. It interests me. Colours also add interest."

"Martha?" said Sandra, stepping closer to the gap in the curtain.

"I am interested in colours," the voice went on. "I'm interested in coloured stripes, and blending edges of rows like rainbows. To blend, one knits two strands together. Strands means yarn. This is a yarn about strands. You can knit two yarns together, but this makes garments bulky. Bulky garments are full of texture."

"Martha?" said Sandra again. She looked through the gap. Martha was lying on her back, staring at the ceiling. Her hands opened and shut as she talked.

"Texture is bumps and lumps, and smooth silky spaces, and knots and curls and knobby buttons. To make different textures you must change purl one knit one. Starting at the star you begin: knit two together, yarn over needle, knit one, yarn over needle, knit two together through back of loop, repeat from star."

Knitting nonsense, thought Sandra.

"Martha," she said, firmly this time. "It's me, Sandra. I've come to see how you are." But the hands opened and shut just the same, and the voice droned on. Sandra looked around for a chair.

"To make a lacy texture of holes and fills, turn around and purl. Pearl is also a kind of colour. Colours are all the colours of the rainbow and the colours between the rainbow colours between. I can never get indigo. Year after year I wait for indigo, but even when the fashion is navy, you never get indigo, the glow, the long slow glow of indigo in the high night sky."

There were no chairs in the room, but Sandra found one in the corridor. She brought it in and sat by the bed. She was loud and deliberate about it, to startle Martha out of this strange intensity. Where was the real Martha, the Martha she knew?

"Why do you knit, Martha?" she asked. Perhaps if she entered her strange world Martha would follow her out. Without missing a beat, Martha answered.

"I knit at night in order to have ease. It's easy to keep order in knitting. Count one, two, three. Simple numbers, knit one purl one, simple knowledge, yarn over needle, slipstitch. Simple notions, simple numbers, easy rows. So easy. Easy does it. Drop a stitch and catch it up again. It's easy to fix mistakes in knitting."

"Martha, look at me! It's me, Sandra."

Martha turned her face toward Sandra, but her eyes were glassy and strange.

"The mind is not like knitting, Sandra. Mistakes in the mind cannot be easily fixed. Knitting is straight, orderly, neat rows with even numbers. But the mind is messy, most uneven. The mind is like a cat in the wool making tangles. You can untangle wool, though a tight knot must be cut. With scissors. Two cuts, either side of the knot made by the cat. Cut. Cat. Cut."

Sandra was frightened now. Martha kept on staring at her, and Sandra met her gaze, but it was hard. She wanted to look away. She wanted to run away, but she couldn't leave her like this.

"They say my mind is tangled, and call me Loopy Loo. The *o*'s in Loo are loops." Martha described large loops in the air with both hands, and looked back toward the ceiling.

"But *o*'s are round and simple, circular. My mind goes round in circles. Oh no, it will not make an *o*. It won't join up: it spirals out and tangents. Spirals and tangents are maths. Maths are like Martha, with bits missing and a spiralling *s*.

Where were the nurses? How could they let someone rave on like this? Sandra poked her head into the corridor but couldn't see anyone. The nurses' station was empty. Uncertainly Sandra went back to her chair.

"My mind shoots into knitting. Bang! Bang! Bang!"

Martha's voice was louder now, the pitch higher. "Which pattern, this pattern, that pattern. Big size little size. Pink wool, blue needles. Black wool is best on white needles. Sharp needles. Sharp needles but a comfortable chair, that's best. It's best to knit."

Martha's voice dropped to a whisper.

"If I knit, I don't get into knots, the loops stay even. If you increase the tension, anything can happen. You must keep the tension even, decrease evenly. Oh, Sandra!"

Sandra jumped.

"Yes, Martha dear, what is it?"

"Oh, Sandra!" she said again. Sandra saw that her eyes were full of tears. "I would like to turn around. On circular needles you don't turn around. You keep going on the same old stitches in the same old direction, round and round and round."

She looked back at the ceiling and clenched her hands.

"Martha! Martha, listen to me." But Sandra didn't know how to continue, and Martha didn't stop.

"Circular needles are good for Fair Isle. When you change rows on circular needles, tie a third strand between the rows. A third strand makes all the difference: you can tell the rows apart. I'm apart, in my apartment. Knitting. A part of knitting. Knitting the next part. Once I knit my name into a garment with no mistakes at all. Won't somebody please fix all my mistakes? My name is

Martha, poor Mad Martha, make no mistake about that."

The voice stopped. Sandra waited for it to start again, but although Martha's breathing was still rapid she had stopped talking. Sandra quietly put the chair back against the wall and crept out.

A DAY later Martha had stopped raving but had retreated deep inside herself. She acknowledged Sandra's presence, but that was all. She still burned with fever. That evening Malcolm, Martha's brother, asked to meet Sandra in the hospital foyer the next day.

Sandra watched him come down the escalator. This had to be her brother—the same oval face, the long chin, the same sandy strawberry look.

"Are you Sandra?" he said while still some yards away, talking to her as though she were on the far side of a ute or a tractor. She nodded and he strode towards her, extending a large square hand that looked as if it could fix anything. He shook her hand and took a step backward. His eyes were clear and curious. She imagined that he'd walk around stock auctions with that same intent look on his face.

"Shall we have coffee?" asked Sandra. "There's a coffee shop up on the fourth floor."

Malcolm stood aside for her at the elevator, gesturing her in ahead of him. He wore a wedding ring, large and solid-looking and shiny. New. Or not worn often. They lined up along the stainless steel counter with their mugs of coffee. Sandra let Malcolm pay.

Malcolm spoke first. "She talks a lot about you. Thanks for all you've done."

Sandra shrugged. "It's no big deal."

"When the hospital rang I thought she'd had another breakdown. She gets this perfectionist streak, can't bear mistakes in her work. She unravels them or starts something else, but she never chucks them out or leaves them behind. Has to carry them everywhere, says she's going to undo them and rework them, but she never does. Well, that's how it used to be, so I thought she'd had another crash. But it's an infection, they say. She's just slow to respond to treatment."

"Do you see her very often?"

"Once a month or so, when I come to the city. But it's hard to tell how she really is sometimes."

Martha had barely mentioned her brother.

"Does she visit you at all?"

"Not often. Christmas sometimes. She doesn't have a car, and getting to our place is awkward. It's a long way. And—she and my wife don't get on. She wants everything to be just as it was, and she tells Penny how to do things— small things, like setting the table—but constantly, so it's irritating. After her husband died—did she tell you she was married?"

Sandra nodded.

"She was very young. They were living in the house

we live in now. It flipped her out. She had to have everything just so, in order to cope. At first she said she had to
have everything right for when he got home—she didn't
accept his death for some months, really—and you could
hardly walk into her place without her trying to tidy up
your shadow. But then it seemed to sink in, and she started
to go out a bit more and began knitting for people in the
neighbourhood. Though she still had this thing about getting things right.

"Anyway, we were all there together. Things came to
a head between Martha and my wife. Martha was making
life hell for Pen, and we suggested she move down here.
She's worse at the farm. Maybe it reminds her of all she's
lost, or maybe it's something from her childhood. It didn't
just start when Manny died; it was there long before that.
And she's been quite happy in town. She enjoys the Art
Gallery and the museums and things like that. She's been
living here fifteen, twenty years now."

He was quite a talker, this brother. He wasn't finished, either.

"She sort of manages, but she still carries her bags.
I don't know if she ever looks in them. She just shoves
things in. Pen emptied them all out once, and Martha just
about killed her. Real catfight. If she's careful she can knit
a whole garment without trouble, but if she gets uptight,
she makes mistakes and goes over the edge.

"Anyway, she told me weeks ago you'd been a good
friend. I just wanted to meet you and fill you in a bit, just in

case anything happens. But it's just her kidneys, they say."

"Kidney infections are serious! And she's been delirious."

"Yes, but that will pass. I know it's bad, but it's more straightforward than the other stuff. She's still got her bags, I see, but that's OK. That's normal. And her temperature's coming down."

"Do you think she might have some kind of delayed reaction after this? Like a breakdown?"

He shrugged and looked at his watch. "Maybe. I don't know." They talked for a few more minutes, then Malcolm stood up.

"Sorry, I have to go. I spent some time with Martha before this, and my parking meter's about to run out." They stood up and he proffered his big hand again. "Thanks for looking after her. It's a relief to know she's got someone like you."

AFTER saying goodbye to Malcolm, Sandra went up to see Martha. She was awake, lying on her side, unnaturally flushed and still on an IV. To Sandra's relief she smiled weakly. Sandra put the box of sweets on the bedside table, next to a vase of irises with a card from Kate and Tony.

"Thanks."

"Shall I unwrap one for you?"

"No. Might puke."

"How are you feeling?"

"Same. Sorry, can't knit. Tried, can't do it."

"Never mind."

"What will you do?"

"Don't know yet." Sandra held herself together and said the right words. "Don't you worry about it. Just get better. Do you need anything from home?"

"Pyjamas. My key's there in the drawer." Martha indicated the drawer with a turn of her head. Sandra opened it and took out a key on a rubber-duck key ring.

"Where are they?"

"Drawers by the bed."

"Anything else?"

"Undies. Next drawer." Talking was an effort, Sandra could see.

"I just had a coffee with Malcolm. He seems nice."

"Yes."

They sat without speaking for a few minutes. Martha's eyes closed at intervals. Sandra stood up and touched her arm with two fingers.

"I'll go now, Martha. Get the staff to ring me if you need anything."

SANDRA made her way up to the sixth floor of the parking station and got into her car. She had parked with her nose to the street and was looking through the safety grille at an office block. If your accelerator got stuck and you rammed the barrier, you would sail through into the street below. Life was full of danger and treachery.

Martha was sick.

She was too sick to finish the knitting in time for the exhibition. Why hadn't Sandra seen it coming? Martha was sick in the body and sick in the head, a perfectionist living on the edge. What person in their right mind went through life lugging three large bags?

Sandra thumped the steering wheel. This is why you don't get involved with strangers in the street. You never know what you are taking on. Now the exhibition was off, and there'd be all that explaining and apologising. And the funds, all the tricky business of money and reporting that went with grants. Martha was a long way from normal health, and it was too late to find new knitters. Damn damn damn.

But below the inconvenience was something worse. The exhibition had been holding her together. She hadn't got over Jack, and she'd landed herself another sick person. She never knew where to draw the line. Here she was, parked outside a hospital again and trying to mount a doomed exhibition. It had all been going so well.

THE drive home took her near Kate's street. She drove past the corner, then changed her mind and went back around the block. Kate opened the door.

"Sandra! What's the matter?"

"Martha's in hospital. The exhibition's off."

"Yes, I saw Cliff when I was shopping, and he told me. How is she? Is she any better?"

"Not really. Kidney infection, py—. Oh, I can't remember. Something nephritis. She's on IV antibiotics but not responding. They think she might have a blockage in the ureter: she's having a scan in the morning. I think she was delirious yesterday—all this crazy knitting talk. And on top of that her brother Malcolm tells me she's in line for a breakdown."

Kate put coffee in front of Sandra.

"Why did he think that?"

"History of mental illness. You know, all those bags she carries. Do you know what's in them?" Sandra laughed grimly. "Her mistakes! I wonder how many of my exhibition garments are stuffed in those bags."

"*Your* exhibition garments?"

"Martha's. Ours."

"I thought she'd finished a lot of garments already."

"Yes, but there's a lot more unfinished. I have no idea what stage they're at." Sandra spilled some coffee and swiped at the wet spot with unnecessary force. "Why couldn't she have told me she wasn't coping?"

"Hold on a minute," said Kate. "Aren't you confusing the issues? One, Martha's sick, and two, the exhibition is affected. The actual work was going all right, wasn't it? She didn't know she was going to get sick."

"She should have told me about her perfectionist streak, that there might be problems."

"But you knew about that. Didn't you?"

"No, how would I?"

"Oh, Sandra, you only have to watch her work! How she concentrates, and how she checks and counts all the time. But she didn't let it affect anything. You were getting the garments. Anyway, I thought the exhibition was mainly for Martha, to showcase her work?"

That's what she'd told Kate. How could she tell anyone why she needed it so much, this little exhibition in a church hall? It had gathered more momentum than she'd expected, but it wasn't that big in the scale of things. Just a funny little project to block the view of the bottomless chasm called Life-Without-Jack. A little project that had grown beyond expectation into something more significant. But even with Kate it was hard to be honest.

"Well, yes, but it's bigger than that. Of course it is. You know what I was trying to do, Kate. Women and work and domesticity. The invisible history, the patching of fragments."

Kate smiled.

"It's never really had much to do with Martha, has it? She was the means to an end. It's always been your project."

"No! It was just as much for Martha! So people could see how brilliant she is."

Kate was silent.

"Kate?"

"As I remember it, you were very keen, and Martha was reluctant, but she did it for your sake. The overseas interest meant it picked up speed, which put the pressure on her even more. But the timelines were tight, right from the start. She's really been struggling. She's been knitting from about nine in the morning until midnight every night. I'm not surprised she's sick."

"Well, why didn't she tell me? Why didn't *you* tell me?"

"She told me in confidence. She didn't want to let you down."

Sandra put her head in her hands.

"So now what? Where does that leave me? Martha's sick, it's all my fault, and we'll have to cancel. Oh, sorry, Jonty, it's all off."

"You don't have to cancel it. Just postpone it. It's only the church hall, after all. There's nothing else coming up, it's not as though it's booked out. Have you sent out the invitations?"

"Not yet."

"Well, a reprint's no big deal. Relax, Sandra, it's not the end of the world. Now, how about staying for dinner? Do you want a glass of red?"

"No. I have to pick up stuff for Martha."

"Ah, so you're looking after her. Good for you. But you can do that later, can't you?"

"No, I've got lectures to prepare."

It's always been your project, Kate had said. Selfish Sandra strikes again. Martha's closed eyes, Jack's face turned away, shutting her out. Retreating inside themselves, where she couldn't reach.

At the door Kate gave Sandra a hug and looked her in the eye.

"You're not such a bad old stick," she said. "Don't be so hard on yourself."

ON THE way to Martha's it started to rain. Sandra stood under the postage-stamp awning at the front door and fished in her handbag for Martha's key on its yellow rubber-duck key ring. The duck waggled at her merrily as she fiddled with the unfamiliar lock. The wind started up again and the rain blew in under the awning at her stockinged legs. Then the key turned, and she was in, into the warm dark, the faint smell of mothballs, and a sudden silence.

She felt for the light switch and turned it on, then edged around the orange horse and looked it full in the face.

"Hello, horse," she said, her voice raspy in the silent room. "Your creator is sick. You won't be going to the show." The horse looked different. It was smiling at her somehow, but what exactly Martha had tweaked to give it that funny look of amusement, Sandra couldn't say. It had grown at the edges, too. Martha had done more work on

the rump, and the saddle shape extended further downward.

Staring around the small room, Sandra realised that
on earlier occasions she had noticed only the more obvious pieces of knitting—the horse, a couple of rugs thrown
over chairs, a cap on a hook by the door. Her attention had
been on finding patterns, taking Martha—and her bags—
shopping. She had never paid proper attention to the
smaller details of Martha's homey little nest.

It was a soft place of curving surfaces, padded chairs,
woven rugs. There were lots of cushions—patchwork,
crochet, knitted, appliqué, woven, embroidered, even a
battered-looking cushion made from tubes of French knitting. Each was beautiful, marrying texture to colour. The
colour of the walls, cream—or was it pale grey or green?
Sandra couldn't tell in this light—made a peaceful foil to
the bright clusters of colour. There was a Bakelite radio, a
relic from the farm, perhaps. Surely Martha wasn't into
buying expensive retro. Facing the radio was an ageing
cane chair, sturdily made, its deep hollow softened with a
cushion of intricate drawn-thread work. A granny rug
hung neatly on its back.

Along the main wall was a miner's seat, the rich
Moroccan coverlet exactly picking up the colours of the
hooked rug below. At one end of the seat—Sandra smiled
in spite of herself—was piled a zoo of tiny animals, a
winking donkey, a tightly knitted miniature python,

a woolly lamb leaning on a regal lion, a happy dog with pink tongue lolling, a little red hen, a whiskered mouse in a tartan waistcoat. At the other end was a fat, squashy cushion embroidered into a friendly elephant, its trunk curled up toward the sultan and his wife and children in the howdah on its back. And tucked into the corner on the floor was a hippopotamus footstool, shaped so that it seemed to rise from the blue carpet as though from water.

Sandra moved through to the kitchen. On the bulletin board were various knitting pictures and patterns. Some she recognised as garments they had chosen for the exhibition—a variation of a Kaffe Fassett jacket in glorious merging stripes, the neck-to-knee woollen bathing suit. But there were others too: a black-and-white portrait of a nun knitting and laughing, a reproduction of a mediaeval knitting Madonna, a mother and child wearing jumpers connected by enormous sleeves. Down one side Martha had stuck the wool samples from wholesale suppliers, their bright tufted rows softening the edge of the board. Below them sprouted a forest of glass-topped pins, and in one corner was a nursery label for a pink rose named Martha. The electricity bill was pinned up too, such a small amount that Sandra wondered if there was an error. On the counter was a loose cluster of knitting needles, as though Martha had been sorting them when she'd been suddenly called away. The only other items on the counter were a small tray of sugar, salt, sauce and vinegar, and a bunch of now wilted yellow dahlias. Sandra, guiltily curious, opened the cupboard near the stove, where she found a neat stack of three saucepans, two casserole dishes with lids, and a lemon squeezer and grater.

In the sink was one dirty teacup. Sandra paused. Should she wash it or let it be? She left it.

Sandra had looked at many such units once when she was searching for an investment property, though none anywhere near so cheerful or innocent. She went back through the living room to the closed door of what she knew would be the smaller bedroom. She pushed open the door and turned on the light. Oh yes, Martha's workroom, the room jewelled with piles of coloured wool, where Martha had brought her to find the pattern books. Sandra looked around properly this time, to take it all in.

The wall opposite the door was taken up with a large window. The blind was up, and Sandra could see nothing except her own reflection. It was like being inside a fish tank. Sandra pulled down the blind and closed the curtains, then turned to look at the room.

By the window were a work table and a high-seated chair, small and straight-backed. A *work* chair. On the table were a couple of folded finished garments. Sandra shook them out, the man's bathing suit, the maroon skirt Martha had been making the night they knitted together. The walls crowded with Martha's pictures observed Sandra's clumsy efforts to refold the garments. It took her some time to get them just as they were.

As she turned to leave, she saw that the back of the

door was also covered with pictures, of animals this time, the smooth sleek lines of dolphins, the intelligent eyes of chimps, a close-up of a lion's paw. With the door shut it would look as though a horde of animals was jammed in the doorway.

Pyjamas. She had come for pyjamas. Sandra left the workroom, shut the door, and entered the main bedroom. The bed was a mess from when Martha had left for hospital. Sandra stripped and remade the bed with clean sheets from a linen cupboard smelling of lavender, put the hot water bottle in the laundry, bundled up the dirty sheets, and put them by the door to take home to wash.

The pyjamas, a pair of red flannelette tartans and another pair covered in whimsical small elephants, were where Martha had told her, in the bedside locker. Martha's undies were full-bodied practical cotton, each pair folded in half and neatly stacked. Sandra wouldn't have wanted anyone looking in her undies drawer.

Did Martha have a dressing gown? The night she had gone in to hospital Sandra had quickly grabbed her coat, but perhaps she would be more comfortable in a gown.

No hooks on the bedroom door. Sandra opened one side of the wardrobe and was flooded with the smell of mothballs. Half a dozen knitted garments, pressed and tidy on their hangers: another skirt for the exhibition, an intarsia jumper of an enormous flannel flower, a man's V-neck sleeveless pullover in grey and blue—more garments than she had expected. A child's jumper with a blue and red train emblazoned on the front, and—what was this? Sandra took it out.

It was a long dress. No—it was a *gown*, knitted in cream wool, a fine lace stitch, and somehow vaguely familiar, surely no more than two-ply. The fabric had a sheen to it, even in this dim light. In Sandra's touch-starved hands it felt soft as petals. At the neck was a triangular insert of diamond lacework, a tiny pearl centred in each diamond. Clustered randomly over the lacework was a delicate appliqué of knitted serrated leaves and open-faced roses.

Sandra lifted the hem toward the light to examine the skirt. It was a pattern she didn't recognise, but at the hem were more roses, hundreds of tiny roses, in the same pattern as the bodice, and edged in a kind of lace. It was the garment Martha had been making at the beach house. What had she called it? Roseheart.

This work made the orange horse, with all its intricacies and cleverness, look coarse and clumsy.

There were no seams; it had been knitted in the round. The full skirt was knitted down from the bodice in a series of graduated increases, so that the whole garment draped to the floor with graceful simplicity. The neck was slightly scooped and lace-edged; the long sleeves, like the body, were seamless. Lace edging at the wrists matched that of neck and hem.

Sandra slipped the dress, soft and warm as a new

spring day, from the hanger. She held it against herself. It was about her size, and from the mirror she could see the length was just right. She suddenly had a great longing to know how it felt to wear such a dress. Would it matter if she tried it on? It was such an intimate thing to do. Would Martha mind? This must be Martha's sales cupboard. Such varied works. Who would have ordered this? A bride, perhaps. Had this job competed with the exhibition pieces?

Sandra's skin craved the full sensation of that dress. Surely it wouldn't matter. It wasn't as though she were going anywhere—she wasn't even leaving the room.

How could plain, stubborn Martha—sick, slightly mad Martha, who didn't dress particularly well herself—create such a garment?

Sandra closed her eyes and let the dress flow through her fingers. It felt so good, she did it several times, then held it to her face. Tears came to her eyes, though she hardly knew why; perhaps it was the baby wool, the hint of tenderness.

Suddenly music burst into the room, only a few bars, followed by silence. Sandra walked around the flat, listening at windows, but heard nothing now except the sound of cars from the main road. It was as though someone had put on a CD, then immediately turned it off. She recognized it, though, the familiar cello query that opened *Invitation to the Dance*. Jack had waltzed her around the kitchen to that. But Sandra had known it even before she met Jack;

as a young teenager she had played the original piano version, her waltz a mechanical ONE-two-three, ONE-two-three, until the teacher begged her to give it her proper attention, to *listen* for the courtesy of the invitation, to be *gracious* in the response, and to *dance* with the sudden surprise of gaiety and frolic.

In a flash of irritability Sandra hung the dress back on the hanger, aware now that her own clothes scratched like sandpaper, that there was no warmth or elasticity in polyester. She opened the other side of the wardrobe. These clothes she recognised, shirts and pants, Martha's knitted jumpers, her plain green waterproof jacket with the big pockets, and there, on the end, a faded chenille dressing gown. Clean and neat and ordinary. Sandra pulled out the dressing gown, folded it, and put it with the other things. After searching, she eventually found a plastic bag in the laundry, hanging on a hook by itself. She would take the clothing to Martha on her way to work.

MARTHA was still not responding to the antibiotics. She heard the doctors and their students having a conference outside her door. She had been moved into a room by herself.

They left and she dozed a little. The cleaner came in, pushing his trolley of mops and cloths and squirters. He smiled at her and went into the bathroom, leaving the door slightly ajar. He was a quiet worker, efficient and unassuming; Martha sensed he took pleasure in his work, in cleaning and ordering and keeping patients comfortable.

He came out of the bathroom and wiped down the adjustable meal table that swung over the bed. Martha watched him without moving. He looked at her and smiled.

"How are you feeling?" he asked.

"Terrible," said Martha miserably. "Hot as hell. And I have terrible nightmares."

"What can I do for you?"

"Make me better, thanks. I'm sick of this. And I'm so tired. I sleep and sleep, but it doesn't make any difference. Everything's hot. Everything hurts. I'm a mess." She felt a tear trickle down the side of her face and into her ear.

The cleaner took her hand and held it for a moment. His hands were sweet and cool.

"Dear Martha," he said. "I'll come back tomorrow."

CLIFF went to see his sister Joyce and asked for a large piece of wrapping paper. Joyce got out her stash of recycled, neatly ironed paper, folded down into an old shoebox.

"What do you want it for, Cliff?"

But he wouldn't say.

She offered him some strong brown paper, suitable for a man.

"No. Something pretty."

"How about this?" Sunflowers, large and yellow bright.

"Nope."

"This?" It was a tricksy piece with rainbow patterns under a silver surface. Cliff had liked a bit of glitz in his youth and thought the paper beautiful, but it wasn't what he was after this time.

"Nope."

"What, then? You choose, for goodness' sake. I don't know what you want! Take whatever you like."

Cliff leafed through them.

"This one." Pale pink. Well, you never could tell. "And I'll be needing some ribbon."

Joyce raised her eyebrows high at him but kept her mouth shut. She opened a cookie tin and offered him a dozen or so neat rolls of ribbon.

Cliff chose pink again, popped the ribbon into his shirt pocket, thanked her, and left. Joyce walked him through the garden to the gate and watched till he was out of sight.

Cliff waited a decent interval, then started picking roses that hung over fences. Some of them seemed determined to stay with the bush. Pity he hadn't thought of scissors, but it was too late now. After the first half dozen he had perfected his technique, quick and efficient, so that he hardly had to slow down as he passed and picked.

In the parklands Cliff sat on a bench to organise his

bouquet. They were good roses, more than thirty of them, better than any florist job. He bunched and rebunched the roses till the arrangement suited him, then folded them into the pink paper. The ribbon was too long, but he made a drooping bow and carried them in the crook of his arm through the city streets to the hospital.

When he got there Martha was sleeping, though she looked restless. Cliff meekly left his roses at the foot of the bed. As he was leaving, a man came along the corridor and spoke to him.

"Would you like to put those roses in water?" he asked.

"Yes," said Cliff, and went back and picked them up again.

The man led him to a small kitchen with a cupboard full of glass jars.

"Take your pick," he said.

Cliff chose a wide-mouthed sturdy jar and took some care arranging the roses. The man watched him until he was nearly finished, then spoke again.

"You must have a beautiful garden."

Cliff looked him in the eye.

"I do," he said. "Adelaide's a beautiful place this time of year."

The man laughed.

"It surely is," he said. "Nice to see someone enjoy it."

MARTHA was still hot. She had heard Cliff put the jar of roses on her bedside cupboard but had kept her eyes closed until he left. It was too much effort to talk. There was a heat deep down inside her belly somewhere, and it was burning her up, burning her inside out, and if the hospital wasn't careful it would get burnt up too. She wasn't sweaty any more, she had no moisture left; it had all cooked out of her like herbs in the oven. She was going to shrivel up like a burnt black sausage and be no good for anything, no good for anything at all. The next time they came to take her temperature they'd find nothing but a little pile of grey ash with a few sticks of bones, like Mary Sherbet said happened at the crematorium. Poor old Martha, they'd say, all burnt up for want of water. Shrivelled herself to death, all those mistakes just like kindling. Spontaneous combustion.

And then she saw the cleaner at the foot of the bed. His appearance had altered, but she knew who he was, all right. Through her feverish eyes he was as hot and burning as she was, but it was different for him, he wasn't burning up, he was just burning, white-hot, a steady flame that she wouldn't normally look at because it was light to burn your eyes out. But they were burning anyhow, so what the heck, she might as well get it over with. As he came closer she could smell his fire; it was hot and sweet and roses somehow, ashes of roses. He was even hotter than she was, his heat was crackling her up inside and out, burning her senses, her common sense, her sensibility, to big black cinders. This was it, then. This was the end. With a huge sigh of relief she gave herself up to whatever was coming next. He leaned over her. She felt the incandescence crackle into her hair, face, body, her dry hands fluttering on the sheet like autumn leaves. Breathe it in, breathe it in, breathe it in. Fire to consume everything.

With his kiss the whole room exploded into flames.

MARTHA, lying on her left side, opened her eyes. Something was missing. Without moving, she felt around inside herself for what it was, like a tongue looking for a rotten tooth that had been extracted. On the pillow next to her face was a hand. It was a left hand, she noticed, the thumb extended toward her. If it was her hand, perhaps the thumb had just slipped out of her mouth; she felt so like a baby waking up from a deep, contented sleep. The thumb moved slightly. Yes, it was her hand, and her thumb, she was making it move, just a tiny bit, like that. The hand was lying on a cotton pillowcase, and the pillow was comfortable, soft but firm, perfect. She was cosy and warm and comfortable and everything was absolutely dandy.

WHEN Sandra came into the hospital late the next day with another set of clean pyjamas, Martha was sitting up in bed eating a boiled egg. The IV tubes were gone.

"Look, all better. Going home tomorrow."

Sandra was astonished at the change. She didn't know what to say.

"This tastes good. Had a sandwich for lunch and now I'm allowed this." Martha tapped the egg with her spoon. "They told me I didn't eat for five days."

"How do you feel?" asked Sandra.

"Good. Really good. I'd go home now, but they want to clear it with the doc in the morning."

On the flower shelf was a big bunch of roses.

"Who gave you those?"

"Cliffy. Poor old bugger thought I was going to kark it and never finish his bed socks."

Sandra couldn't help herself. "Are you up to knitting?"

"Sure. No worries. Look here." Martha reached over into the side cupboard for a plastic bag, but couldn't quite reach. She hopped out of bed, sprightlier than Sandra had ever seen her, and arrayed pieces of knitting on the bed. There it was, the baby's layette in the white shell pattern, dress, jacket, bonnet, bootees, undershirt, soakers, though some seams were not yet stitched. The last piece was still on the needles, all but finished. Beautiful work, fine and even.

"When did you start this?"

"Oh, in that last week before I got sick, but it went wrong, so I didn't show it to you. Then I got sick. I kept trying to fix it, and it got worse and worse, and I had a massive headache, so I stuffed it in one of my bags. I was so hot, I thought I was going to shrivel up. Then something happened." Martha looked so distant for a minute that Sandra felt alarmed, but she continued in an ordinary voice.

"When I woke up yesterday I was better. This lot of knitting was folded up at the foot of the bed, and there was nothing wrong with it."

"So who fixed it?"

Martha shrugged. "Don't know."

Martha took another bite of egg. Sandra looked around the room. Something was missing.

"Where are your bags now?"

Martha shrugged.

"Don't know that either." She tore open the pepper packet on her tray.

"Aren't you worried about them?"

"No. Good riddance."

"Martha, you never let them out of your sight!"

Martha took another bite of toast and chewed solidly, looking at Sandra.

"Do you know what was in them? Rubbish. Things I'd been trying to fix my whole life."

"But where are they now?"

"Don't know. Gone, anyway. Just as well. I could never have got rid of them. All that waste, all that time and energy."

"Do you have any idea who took them?"

"The cleaner, maybe."

"The cleaner?"

"Yes. He can knit, I reckon."

Sandra shook her head.

"Martha, I hate to say this, but I don't think you've got things straight."

"Sandra, look at me! I felt like I was dying. And now"—Martha gestured with both hands, trying to find words—"I'm better. Head's clear. I can get on with things, like these baby clothes."

"There weren't any mistakes?" Sandra asked cautiously.

"Not when I got them back, though I've made one since. I lost a stitch low down in the rib, and when I got to the top it was too tight to knit all the way up. But I didn't chuck it in this time, I just threaded a needle and sewed it so it wouldn't come undone. It's not perfect, but it doesn't matter. I'm never going to be perfect."

Sandra shook her head in disbelief.

"I know. I couldn't say that before. I was all in a knot. But it's only knitting, to keep people warm, so what's the point? And I don't have to lug those bloody bags around any more. I'm blowed if I'm going to get new ones." Her voice cracked a little, but she was smiling. Was she teary? Sandra couldn't be sure. Then Martha frowned.

"It wasn't you, Sandra? Was it? Took the bags away?"

Sandra shook her head. Martha looked relieved.

"Must have been the cleaner. Look out for him, Sandra. I reckon you'd like him if you gave him a chance."

IT WAS nearly Easter. Sandra had taken Martha home earlier in the day and was sharing a glass of wine with Kate before dinner. Tony was working late.

"I want to ask you something," said Sandra.

"Fire away."

"How was I when Jack died?"

"What do you mean?"

"I can't remember it objectively. How did I behave?"

"Like anyone would in extreme circumstances."

"Oh, come on, Kate. Did I make an idiot of myself?"

"There's no right or wrong way to grieve. You have to find your own way. Nobody minds, for goodness' sake."

"What about Jack? I mean, how was I with Jack?"

Kate took another mouthful of wine. "Just what exactly are you asking me?"

"Did I give him a hard time?"

"Oh, Sandra."

"But did I? I was so stressed out, I don't know what I was like."

"You were a bit—rigid. Look, I don't know if this is very helpful."

"Kate, I haven't got Jack to front me any more. Now help me sort this out. What do you mean, rigid?"

"Pour me another glass."

Sandra poured.

"Keep me company," said Kate, gesturing toward Sandra's glass.

"No. I'll fall asleep. Talk."

Kate sighed. "You're just intense. You've always been intense. It's just how you are. You're passionate about things. And when the pressure's on, you get anxious and try to control things. And of course, when you had a husband dying, you got very anxious indeed. Of course you did."

"Did Jack say anything?"

"No."

"Did Jack ever complain about me to you?"

"No, he never did. He was so loyal to you it drove me mad."

"So I did give him a hard time?"

"Yes, you did. You give everybody a hard time when you're like that. Look, we all do it, it's just the expression that's different. You turn into a control freak; I get moody and sullen and spiteful. We all do it, it just comes out in different ways."

"Was I bossy with Jack?"

"Probably. It's your pattern. But he'd had it for twenty-eight years, it would hardly have been a new experience. He had his own way of resisting. And maybe he just wanted to be by himself at the end."

They finished their wine and carried the pilaf outside to eat in the fading light. Kate was talking now, about Tony and Jeremy, about menopause, about the movie she'd seen last week. Sandra smiled and answered at appropriate intervals.

Bossy with Jack. She hadn't even let him die in peace.

Kate saw her to her car, her face anxious. Now that Sandra had decided to go, she was in a hurry to leave. She slammed the car door just as Kate leaned toward her to say something. Kate made a face, but it took a few seconds before Sandra realised that she had slammed the car door on Kate's thumb.

"Oh, Kate! I'm so sorry!"

Kate was white, her face strained. Sandra took her inside.

"Is there anything I can do?"

"No, no. Don't worry, Sandra. Just an accident. Go on, go home. I'm all right." Kate was rocking a little, holding her thumb up to her cheek.

"Go on! Tony will be home soon. You can't do anything."

Sandra drove home with her eyes smarting.

SANDRA felt worse as Martha's health improved. Every night she lay in bed wide-eyed, staring at the rectangle of faint light that was the window. She could feel herself in the vortex, circling inward toward facts she didn't want to face.

She got out of bed, pulled a woollen jumper over her pyjamas, forced her feet into socks and ugg boots, went out to where the cold moon shone in the pool. A magpie sang out and a possum scrambled up the fence and thudded on the shed roof.

The moonlit garden was thick with past conversations. The house, too, the whole place seething with memories: loving, fighting, jeering, weeping, silences, jolts of tenderness. She and Jack had lived here ever since they married, determined to stay based in Adelaide, renting the house out while they lived overseas.

Around the pool stood Jack's fruit trees, silent sentinels planted for special occasions: the plum, apricot and peach for each of Jack's three scholarly works, various citrus trees for wedding anniversaries. Jack had been a fruit fanatic, gradually replacing nonfruiting trees and shrubs with an edible garden. The house was built on a double block. Bit by bit Jack had claimed the backyard for his garden; the front he had dedicated to indigenous plants for the birds. He experimented with exotic fruits, nurtured bushtucker plants, erected trellises for berries and vines to cover sheds and tanks. Spring was pink and white with apple and nut blossom, in autumn pomegranates hung red and heavy by the gate, and after leaf fall a solar system of persimmons swung around the bare black trunk. Jack was never happier than when his hands were deep in compost or bringing her platters of home-grown fruit.

When she was younger, Sandra had been too impatient for gardening. There were too many variables — soil, insects, rootstock, weather. In its first year the almond tree had been covered in little green nuts. Then Jack had gone to a conference and Sandra had forgotten to water it, around the corner as it was, out of the daily line of sight. Most of the baby almonds had withered and dropped, and birds had decimated the rest. But Jack, though disappointed, had proudly brought her the small handful of surviving almonds the following autumn.

Sandra, less knowing then, had looked at them and burst into tears, accused him wildly of heaping coals on her head, and slammed into her study.

Poor Jack. He'd never had an easy time of it.

Now, with the cold slats of the garden seat pressing into her warm flesh, all she could remember was how she had pushed and pulled at him. Even in the garden she had been imperious, insisting that he shift the hole for a tree over a few feet, wanting lettuces sown in straight rows, pulling out a tomato he was nurturing because it had sprung up next to a rose bush. And at the end, opening curtains and windows for fresh air when he preferred darkness, insisting that he rest when he was wakeful, plumping his pillows, rubbing his pressure spots when he would rather have lain quietly. Loving him too hard and all wrong.

What she had done with Martha was more of the same, though less intense perhaps. Driving and pushing, organising, creating projects with a purpose, achieving her own ends. And for what? To keep the fear at bay.

Fear. The word had come spontaneously. What did she fear? Nothing, really. Except being alone with her own ugliness.

APRIL

FOR SANDRA the week before Easter had been packed. When the supermarket closed the evening before the Friday holiday, she was last in line at the checkout.

Martha had been home for three days; surely now it would be all right to ring.

Martha, sounding chirpy, pre-empted Sandra's big question. "Look, Sandra, I just can't do it by the date we set. It will have to be later in the year. I'm really sorry, but I just about drove myself crazy with the pressure."

Although Sandra had been expecting this, she was still unprepared for the wave of disappointment and self-pity that swept over her.

"Oh, we would have been all right if you hadn't got sick." The edge of bitterness in her voice dismayed her, but she didn't seem able to stop. "It was just bad luck. We were organised enough up until then." A subtle shifting of blame. She despised herself for it, but Martha's response was mild.

"No, we were both too pressured. It wasn't fun any more. And it was spoiling our friendship. I was starting to hate you for making me work so hard. But it was my fault, too—I said yes. I don't hate you now. I just feel sorry for you. You're like a sheepdog with a mob of sheep and no pen to put them in."

Sandra hung up as soon as she decently could. She found a few withered vegies in the fridge and tried to make them edible. She hadn't finished her shopping; she'd have to go to a seven-day supermarket tomorrow. She couldn't find anything good on TV either, only old reruns of bad biblical movies. Nothing to distract her from herself.

On Good Friday Sandra woke cold as ice. She had clenched her teeth in the night; her jaw ached, her neck was stiff, her knees would not bend properly. Perhaps she was getting the flu. She stayed under the shower a long time, but the marrow was frozen in her bones. It was going to be a wet and windy weekend.

Last Easter she had spent on her own, wandering and sad. On Saturday, the six-month anniversary of Jack's death, she had tackled a backlog of paperwork to keep herself busy. Kate and Tony had asked her to dinner, but the food tasted like sawdust. She had excused herself early and gone home to lie on her bed and stare blankly at the ceiling. The Easter before that she had taken Jack to the sea, where they had walked among the old chipped rocks. Jack was wrapped in an overcoat and hunched against the wind, but they both enjoyed the crash and boom of the breakers, the spray tickling their faces, the timeless salty tang in the air. They had spent the long evenings by an open fire playing chess and reading. And had spoken for the first time of the reality of his dying.

But this Easter she had no plans. The four days looked long and bleak.

Good Friday. Kate had invited her to attend the Easter services, but she had declined. Had she ever been to a Good Friday service? Not as an adult. Well, perhaps she would go after all; she'd surprise Kate. She must not succumb to self-pity. She sat stiffly at the cold breakfast table drinking coffee, with toast and marmalade that was sickly sweet. The morning paper was a mass of advertising.

As she backed her car out of the driveway, a middle-aged couple stopped on the footpath to let her pass. They were talking animatedly and laughing under their big umbrella. The weather was not bothering them.

It was too early for the service, much too early. She should have stayed longer at home, turned on the heater, warmed the house. But she had inherited a family frugality; she didn't believe in wasting resources. She rarely turned on the heat before work.

It started to rain again. Gutters clogged with autumn leaves became little rivers. She didn't want to go into the church too soon, into that strange community Kate talked about so often, into the bustle of baskets and bosoms, the cheerful setting out of milk jugs and sugar bowls and trays of buns ready for the oven. Although she hated driving in the rain, she went out of her way, around the perimeter of the city, and got to the church a couple of minutes late, though the service hadn't started. She took a program and sat near the back, tucked into the aisle end of a pew. There was a draft under the old swinging door. She wished she had her ugg boots on instead of shoes.

Well toward the front, on the far side of the church, she saw Martha's red head bobbing about. Newly back from hospital, she was enjoying enthusiastic greetings from friends. She had been missed.

The service began. Sandra stood, sat, stood, sat, mouthed words. Behind her a husband and wife sang in practiced unison, the wife a natural alto. Sandra could hear her own voice, fluttery as paper, insubstantial. Her hand ached; she was holding the order of service in a pincer grip. Her whole body was tightened, shut and protective, somehow far away. She wanted to leave, slip out the back and go home, but she didn't have the energy for that, didn't want to be noticed and perhaps pitied.

At the front of the church was a rough wooden cross, eight feet high, draped with purple. Close by, on the communion table between the bread and the wine, was a large round bowl of dark red roses in full flush. It was well done, simple and dramatic. Meaningful, probably, if you had feelings.

The pastor was speaking now, saying those hard rude Christian words, sin, guilt, shame, sickness, death, blood. It was a hard God they worshipped. The God who gave and took away. Sandra had read the Bible once but had not been convinced. She was not like Job, who had suffered loss and grief and could still bless God. When Sandra got to heaven she would pick a bone with God, have it out, tell him off for giving so much joy and snatching it back.

Kate was leading communion. She took her place, saying words that were vaguely familiar, breaking the loaf. A tall, plain woman with big hands tearing a loaf of bread. The crust was thick. It was an effort, she had to pull hard; Sandra saw the crust crack and crumble, the thickened underbelly pull apart.

This is my body, broken for you, said Kate. Fragile bodies, prone to fatigue, vulnerable to bacteria, succumbing to the civil war of cancer. Dead bodies. Two more suicide bombs had gone off this week. Soft fleshy bodies ripped apart, embedded with fragments of metal, bits of cars and buses, the irony of carpenter's nails. It wasn't fair. Death was everywhere. When Sandra got her scrap of bread she had trouble swallowing.

Kate was holding the cup. *This cup is the new covenant in my blood, which is poured out for you.*

There was a disturbance at the front. Martha was

standing, edging past the other people in the row. Her jacket caught on something, she had to stop and unhook herself. People who had been praying looked up, then looked down again as though caught out. Martha was wearing her clumpy shoes, and her footsteps were not hushed by the red carpet.

Martha walked steadily toward Kate and stood directly in front of the communion table. She nodded to Kate, put her hands under the heads of the roses, and pulled the whole arrangement out of the bowl. She tugged off the green florist's block still sticking to the stems and dumped it back in the vase. She turned, faced the congregation, and began to walk up the left aisle. As she went, she tore off a handful of rose petals and scattered them over the heads of the people. Then another handful. In the great and astonished silence Sandra could hear the roses being torn from their stems.

Sandra looked back at Kate, seated again, and saw her nod to the organist, who began to play. She was allowing it. Kate was going to let Martha do this bizarre thing.

After initial awkwardness Martha developed a kind of grace. She was moving quietly now, tearing and scattering. Petals were falling everywhere, on heads and pews and laps, into babies' prams, onto the floor. A couple of petals fell on the organ keys. Kate stood again and began to follow Martha, offering the cup to the congregation as she went.

Martha was coming closer. Sandra stared down at

hands clenched in her lap. The skin was white, blue veins clear on the back, like fissures in marble. She didn't want to make eye contact with Martha, didn't want to see, didn't want to participate. But she had only two alternatives: to submit or to rush headlong out of the place, which would be even more difficult. Sandra stayed where she was. She was afraid that Martha would speak to her in front of all these people.

It was utterly ridiculous to be so tense. It was only Martha.

Only Martha. Only Martha with her thick, warm body, her big bear hugs, her soft shawls and socks and scarves that tangled into you in spite of yourself. Big soft Martha, with no protection except her soap-smelling skin, open and vulnerable to Sandra's hard glass edge.

Sandra waited for the roses, for their shredded petals and thorny stems.

Martha was close now. Sandra could see a blur of deep red steadily advancing out of the corner of her eye. But Martha did not stop or acknowledge her in any way. A rose petal landed on the back of one of Sandra's clenched hands, another on her knee. She stared at her hand, the dark red on her white skin, the petal with its own tiny veins radiating toward the outer edge, the strong sure curve of it. Harmless, after all. She held it, soft and smooth, against her upper lip, crushed it to inhale its sweetness. Ashes of roses. Ashes to ashes. Dust to dust.

She could hear Kate whispering as she administered the communion cup. Then it was next to her in Kate's large hands, proffered. Sandra saw Kate's bruised thumb, the nail already black.

"Drink deeply of the cup, Sandra."

Sandra hesitated, then took the chalice. The hot blood of life.

The chalice was cold at her lips, the taste rich and sweet. But then unexpected heat, fire pouring down her throat to her empty belly, as though she were drinking molten metal. The fire spread, radiating outward, burning, consuming, spreading in a great conflagration, taking hold of her torso, licking down her arms and her legs. She felt herself give way before it, bow to the white-hot heat. She was paper, she was grass, she was a flaming tree. She was glass melting in the furnace.

SANDRA had lost track of the service. What came next? Rose petals were everywhere, but when she looked up again, she found herself focusing on the bare rose sticks unceremoniously pushed back in the vase.

She stared at them. Stripped, beaten, dead. What had been, what might still be if someone took those spiky dead things and planted them in good soil.

Sandra began to weep then, discreetly at first, hot tears in her tissue, but the tissue was totally inadequate. She groped blindly for her bag. The tears kept falling, running out of her eyes, squirting down her face. Her meagre supply of tissues was soon used up. She put her head in her hands. Her shoulders were shaking and she was making unfamiliar noises.

The service was over. People began to move and leave.

Inside Sandra a dam still swelled until she could no longer hold it back. She kept her head down, sobbing in earnest now, water streaming out of her, bursting from her eyes and nose and mouth, great gouts of it, an unstoppable flood. "Bawling her eyes out"—that's what they used to say at school. She was bawling her eyes out, and she hardly knew why. Her tears were making little marks on her skirt. Her makeup must have washed off long ago.

A woman came and sat next to her, close, shoulder to shoulder, and waited patiently while the tears subsided, but Sandra couldn't look at her; she couldn't look at anybody. This is what other people did in those other churches, the emotional ones, where they lost control of themselves and had strange ecstatic looks on their faces. Sandra didn't feel ecstatic. She felt acutely embarrassed, and wet. Behind that, part of her was reeling away into some strange and unfamiliar orbit.

"Here," said Martha's voice. A neatly ironed hankie, old-fashioned soft cotton with a lace edge, was pushed into Sandra's hand.

"Thanks," said Sandra, mopping at her face.

"We're having buns out the back."

"Thanks," Sandra said again, not looking at Martha, but glad of a hedge against someone more inquisitive.

"Do you want me to bring you coffee and a bun?"

"No." Sandra wiped the back of her hand across her nose like a child. Nearly everyone had gone now. She stood up, still avoiding Martha's eyes.

"I think I'll just go home, if you don't mind. I'll catch up with you later." She walked quickly to her car.

LATER that afternoon, warm from soup and toast and her heated house, Sandra turned on the computer, opened her e-mail program and clicked on the folder called "Jack". Time for the plunge. The window opened, showing all his messages from the year before he died, interchanges while they were both at work, an ebb and flow of conversation, some of it meaningless now without context. Iceberg tips of their relationship.

How was your seminar? Thinking of you.

Lunch with Spack. Love to you, he said.

A giant slog today. Bored. Kangaroo Island for the long weekend?

This morning one of my students came and asked for an extension. She's only 19. Her partner had suicided. She wept and wept in my office and I found some tissues. Young enough to be our daughter, and

I wanted to put my arms around her but protocol persists. What would you have done with one of your young men? The same I suspect. Sometimes I wish we had adopted kids. All this love with nowhere to go.

Was she game to see what she had written him? She opened "Sent/Jack". 349 messages.

No time to shop. Please pick up attached list for our curry night with Kate and Tony. Any coriander left in the garden? I'll have to make it tonight, my only free night. Or do you want to cook?

Dear Jacko Can't find the parking fine. Did you pay it already?

Hot flush score = 32. Male menopause must be a breeze.

Two students were at it in the stairwell and the VC, taking a shortcut, found them. Brightened us all up.

Oh Jacko! Such a lovely day we had yesterday. I keep thinking of that big basket of glowing peaches. Thank you, thank you. All my love, X

Holidays, shopping lists, days shared, love and kisses. She had loved him. She had loved him. She must remember that.

September

It was the first day of spring.

The garments were mounted, the spotlights were on, the speeches would soon begin. The crowd at the exhibition milled around, laughing and smiling, nodding as they pointed to items in the catalogue. The mood was set by the extraordinary orange horse in the foyer, Martha McKenzie's current work in progress. Sandra had written a snappy little piece about twentieth-century horses, tying it to the Light Horse Brigade and the war comforts. It was stretching the connection, she knew, but the horse was a crowd-pleaser, especially for those jaded by too many Friday-night openings.

Martha and Cliff stood in a corner by the kitchen door, mesmerised by the bright lights, the elegance of the crowd, and the transformation of Martha's knitting into magnetic works of art. The wooden floorboards of the church hall gleamed golden. It doesn't look like a church hall at all, thought Martha, but like a proper gallery.

"Looks great, Mattie," said Cliff. He might have been referring to her work, but they were both watching Sandra talking to Kate. Sandra was laughing and wearing high heels, a tight green dress and plenty of makeup. Glittering, Martha said to herself, Sandra is glittering.

"Don't stare, Cliff," she said, but she was telling herself, too, as she righted her wine glass, which had tipped to a precarious angle.

A man wearing a dark grey shirt came in. Martha recognised the body before she saw the face; the set of the shoulders and the neatly contained walk brought instant recall from her memory bank. She had once studied him closely. Now he was different, diminished, an aging psychiatrist out of context, pretending to examine a baby's layette in the middle of a church hall.

She hadn't seen him for thirty years, but it was him, all right, same size and shape, his hair barely grey, a trim little man with a smallish head. The beard was gone, but he still smiled that silly half smile.

She excused herself from Cliff and went to the kitchen to find a plate. It took her a while to find the particular plate she wanted. She piled it generously with assorted breads and cheeses, slices of pickled red pepper and marinated eggplant. Everyone else was using paper napkins, taking tiny portions, mere nibbles, even though it was almost dinnertime. It was wonderful food, she had never seen such food in her life. Why weren't they enjoying it more?

As she approached him she saw that the piercing dark eyes that had frightened her so much no longer knew who she was.

"Here you are, sir," she said. "I got this for you." She smiled broadly and thrust the plate at him. She remembered from hospital gossip that his wife's name was Marguerite, that she had ebony hair and red lips like Snow White.

IN A moment between conversations, Sandra looked for Martha. There she was, offering a man a plate of food. She was wearing a finely knitted swing jacket that Sandra had never seen before, a perfect fit and flattering to her full figure, with twined intarsia roses down each side of the front and asymmetrically placed around the neck and across the sleeves. The rose pattern was not large, and on someone else the jacket might have looked hopelessly old-fashioned, but on Martha tonight it was just right, bohemian and beautiful. She wore no makeup, but her face was soft and shining, with spots of colour in her cheeks. Her hair was up, though wisping undone here and there. Martha caught Sandra's eye across the shoulder of the man in the grey shirt and winked.

"Do I know you?" Dr Gladstone asked.

"I might have met you many years ago," she said,

remembering the slumped circle, the vacant eyes, the erratic behavior. How little he had understood.

"What, at some conference?"

"Maybe."

Martha knew his style of conversation. She saw that his eyes were still small and narrow, that the half smile still masked power tricks. She knew that when he wanted to close the conversation he would take her arm just so and squeeze it gently before moving away. They were about the same height, and she looked back at the dark eyes as hard as they looked at her.

"Do you know the exhibitors?" he asked, juggling the old patterned china plate into his left hand.

"Yes," said Martha, "I do."

"I don't know anything about this kind of thing, but my wife says it's very fine work."

"Yes. The knitting's not bad, but the brains behind it is Sandra, Sandra Fildes. That woman over there." She pointed. "The one in the green dress. Some of these pieces are original; others are historically authentic reconstructions. All are linked with a rich counterpoint of text." A quote from the brochure, unopened in his hand. He looked impressed.

"What's your line of work?" Martha asked boldly.

"I'm a doctor."

"Oh," said Martha. "A GP?"

"No." He laughed. "Don't collapse on me. I wouldn't know what to do. I'm a psychiatrist."

"Well, fancy that." Martha paused. "But if I had a mental illness, you could fix that?"

"There are a lot of variables," he said warily. "But we would try. There are some wonderful drugs these days."

Martha leaned forward and took hold of his arm above the elbow, gently but firmly.

"See your plate, doctor? It's a bit cracked—there, by the pink rose under the eggplant." She took hold of the opposite edge between her thumb and forefinger, so he couldn't let go without it falling, and twisted it around so he could see the crack.

"Do you reckon you could mend that?"

He was not comfortable, but he tried to humour her. "I don't think so. Once cracked, always cracked, I'm afraid."

"Ah," said Martha. "And what about cracked people? Crackpots?"

He looked at her then, hard, but there was still no recognition in his eyes.

"I mean," Martha went on, "it's still a good plate. Quite pretty, really. You didn't even see the crack at first. You only saw the food on it."

"Do I know you?" He took a step backward.

"No, I don't think so. See, if you concentrate on the crack, you'd never use it. You might even chuck it in the bin. But it's still pretty, and it's still useful. And anyway, the crack means it's got a story to tell."

He glanced around.

"Do you know, doctor?" She stepped back again.

"I reckon doctors should listen to their patients."

Her hand was still on his arm, but he laughed a little. "Of course," he said. "The patient's perception is very important."

"Well, I'm glad to hear that. Do you know—" Martha paused. She didn't need to justify herself to this little man. Just as he moved to disengage himself, she tightened her grip momentarily above his elbow, then gave him a little push in the direction of the drinks table.

"Excuse me, Dr Gladstone. I just remembered, I've left someone stranded in the kitchen. Please go on and enjoy yourself." From the corner of her eye she saw him scoop up a glass of red and disappear into the crowd.

Back by the kitchen door Cliff was leaning against some shelving like a multicoloured question mark. He was wearing the knitting-machine vest over an electric blue shirt. His aftershave was overpowering.

"So who's the competition?" asked Cliff.

"Not my type," said Martha.

"You say that about everybody," said Cliff. "But who is he?"

"Oh, a bloke I knew years ago. Ran a therapy group. Still wet behind the ears back then. Tried to trick people into doing what he wanted for their own good. If he talked to you, he'd probably try to make you live in a house. Never had a clue, poor sausage."

"I *am* going to live in a house," said Cliff.

Martha raised her eyebrows.

"I'm moving in with Joyce. You know, my sister. Her heart's worse. She needs help with the gardening, and someone to keep an eye on her. I'm getting past camping out. Too stiff and sore in the mornings."

It was time for the speeches. Martha checked behind the kitchen door. Yes, the bag was still there, the new carpetbag that snapped shut like a crocodile and never let anything out.

Tony, master of ceremonies for the evening, was enjoying himself, cracking a few jokes to the sound man, introducing himself to the minister for the arts. He beckoned Martha, but she shook her head. Tony came over to see what the matter was.

"I don't want to make a speech."

"They'll want to hear from you, Martha. Look around you! Everyone is enjoying your knitting!"

"I told Sandra I don't want to speak."

"Well, just come over for a minute. The minister wants to meet you."

"Hello, Martha," said the minister, a tall woman who extended a hand heavy with jewellery. "This is wonderful, just wonderful. All the detail! However do you find the time?"

"I get up in the morning and I do it," said Martha.

The minister laughed. "Well, so do I, but I wish I could see this level of achievement for the hours I put in!

Congratulations. This work is superb. You must be very pleased and proud." She spoke to Martha for a few minutes more and then moved on. Martha went back to the kitchen to check on her bag.

From her position by the kitchen door, Martha watched the minister open the exhibition. When Sandra finally took the microphone, Martha saw that she was glowing, that some kind of light shone under her skin. Sandra was speaking now, and the words streamed out of her mouth like music. Martha could hear them rising and falling like the sound of flowing water, sometimes slow and smooth, sometimes laughing like a waterfall. Word knitting, thought Martha, words all knitted together to warm your heart like a song. And she detected a new strand woven in with the rest, the sparkle of Sandra having fun.

But now Sandra was saying words with "Martha" knitted into them, and people were turning around and nodding at her, Martha, and they all were smiling.

"So I owe a lot to Martha," Sandra was saying. "Not only for the great contribution she made in providing many of the garments for this exhibition, but because of her commitment to me as a friend.

"Many of you knew Jack. I still miss him terribly, of course, but Martha and others have helped me see that there is a broader fabric, a larger pattern. Please come up here, Martha, so everyone can see who did this wonderful work."

"Wait," said Martha.

"Please, Martha."

"I'm coming," said Martha. "I just have to get something." She ducked through the kitchen door and came out with the carpetbag. The crowd gave way before her as she went up to Sandra and put out her hand for the microphone.

"I wasn't"—she paused as she heard her own voice echo through the mike—"I wasn't going to say anything at all. But I want to give Sandra a present, to thank her for everything. Without her this whole thing would never have happened." She handed Sandra the carpetbag and the microphone.

"Open it."

"Now?"

Martha nodded. Sandra handed the mike to Tony and the crowd strained to see as she unfastened the clasp and took out a large white box.

"Here," said Martha, putting her hands under it for support. "Now you undo the ribbon."

Sandra untied the blue ribbon and took off the lid. Inside was something wrapped in tissue paper. Sandra reached in and took hold of the garment as the tissue paper drifted away. From Sandra's hands poured a length of exquisite lace knitting in the shape of a dress. Those at the front held their breath for a moment. Cameras flashed. Even those further back could see from the lightness and elegance of the drape that this glorious white garment was the jewel of the exhibition.

Sandra, feeling its familiar warmth, looked up in wonder at Martha's smiling face.

Martha took the mike back from Tony.

"It's the best thing I've ever made," she said to the crowd. "So I think she should put it on, don't you?"

"Absolutely," Tony called out. The guests laughed in assent.

Martha was reaching into her carpetbag again.

"So I brought her a changing room." She flapped open a large curtain and gave one end to Tony. "Where's Kate? Here, Kate, please hold this." Kate stepped forward to take the other end.

"Now we'll just pop behind here, and Sandra can try on her new dress. Tony, make sure you face the other way!" The guests laughed again.

But Sandra baulked.

"No, I can't, Martha. Not here. Not like this. Please."

Martha's face fell.

"Don't you want it?"

"Oh, Martha, I love it!" *Love it!* shouted the sound system. Sandra switched the microphone off.

"Martha, it's so beautiful. It's such a generous gift. I don't know what to say. But it's special. I need to be private about it." There were tears in Sandra's eyes.

"Oh!" said Martha. "Is that all? That's all right, then."

She took the microphone back from Sandra and flicked the switch on.

"Sorry to disappoint you, folks. You're not going to see it on her after all. But we'll give you a preview." She took the dress and held it up against Sandra by the shoulders, moving around behind her so everyone could see. Kate gave her end of the curtain to Tony and began clapping. The appreciation gathered momentum. The crowd cheered and whistled.

"OK, that's it," said Martha, when the noise subsided. "If you want a closer look we'll hang it from this curtain rail. Now that's the end of the speeches. There's more food and drinks, so please help yourselves."

"Who's running this show?" asked Sandra, recovering enough to laugh.

"Us," said Martha. "You and me."

IT WAS a late night. Sandra, Kate, and Martha had done most of the catering themselves, and there was a lot to clean up. Much to Martha's amusement, Sandra changed into sneakers and ran around collecting glasses in her shimmery green dress. Sandra and Kate washed up. Martha repacked Sandra's new dress in its tissue paper, then swept the hall floor. Kate offered to take Martha home, but Sandra wanted to do it herself.

At Martha's front gate Sandra turned off the engine.

"Martha, it was a great success. Thank you so much

for all your hard work over the months. And I owe you an apology."

"It's OK, Sandra."

But Sandra rattled on. "I know I pressured you too much. I said I was doing it for you, but it was for me, really. I just get fixated on things; I don't see that people around me are hurting. You got so sick. I'm really sorry for the pain I caused you. I really am."

"Sandra, it's all in the past."

But Sandra couldn't stop. "Anyway, you should do really well now. Those garments created a lot of interest — and people loved the horse. And the dress! The dress! Did you see how people were drawn to it? Oh, Martha, it's such an extravagant gift. I don't deserve it. I don't know how to thank you."

Martha opened her car door, got out, then leaned back in and kissed Sandra on the cheek.

"Sandra, it takes two to tango. I should have looked after myself better. And about that dress; make sure you put it on. It was always meant for you. It's for wearing, that dress, even if you don't go out in it. But you must wear it."

Sandra would have kept talking, yabbering on, but Martha shut the car door firmly and let herself through her own front door without looking back.

The house was cold, so Sandra turned on the heating. She was still buzzing; there was no way she would sleep yet.

She ran a long deep bath and soaked. When she got out, her skin was as rosy and soft as a child's. She dried herself and walked naked through the warm house to where Martha's box still sat on the kitchen table. She untied the blue ribbon a second time and took out the dress.

Fine and light and soft as it was, the dress had more substance than Sandra remembered. Carefully, shyly almost, she let it fall over her head. She felt the shift of balance as it settled around her, the shoulders perfectly in place, the sleeves exactly the right length, the firm enfolding of her bosom, the easy draping to the touch of warmth at her ankle.

The dress held her.

She walked slowly back to the bedroom. The dress gathered around, propelled her forward to where the feathers flew upward on the walls. In the mirror she saw immediately that some transformation had taken place. Something rigid and unyielding had softened and become beautiful.

She did a small pirouette, watching herself in the mirror. It was dangerous, this dress: it made you feel like a princess.

It took her a long time, but in the end she found it, Jack's CD of Weber's *Invitation*. She put the disc in the player and stood in the centre of the living room, listening, with tears in her eyes, to the courteous invitation of the cello, the woodwind's cautious response. She hardly knew whether to laugh or weep. The cello persisted; it was almost time for the waltz. Sandra took a deep breath, curtsied her acceptance and stepped into the pattern of the dance.

ACKNOWLEDGEMENTS

A book is never written in isolation. My thanks to Russell for love and grounding, and always believing this time would come; to my children, David, Danny, Michael and Elisabeth for love, laughter and expanding my horizons; to Jane Rosenman, Bob Wyatt, Peg Anderson and Nicola Young for incisive editing; to Nicholas Jose for great kindness and true mentorship; to the University of Adelaide's Creative Writing program, particularly Tom Shapcott for astonishing availability and sound preparatory instruction and Susan Hosking for friendship, challenge, unstinting support and quinces; to Joy Harris and her team, literary agents extraordinaire; to Julie Watts for holding open the door and to Clare Forster for welcoming me in; to the South Australian Writers' Centre, especially Barbara Wiesner, for being there; to Holly Story ("Dolly Varden"), Anne Farren ("Shiro Kuro" man's shirt), Halka Marsáková ("Lace Raincoat"), Ruby Brilliant ("And Death"), Lindsay Obermeyer (jumper with fifteen-foot sleeves), Bronwen

Sandland ("Housecosy") and photographer Reg Morrison ("Knitter") for rich inspiration; to Mary Jose, Kay Lawrence, Neville Carlier and Eric Jorve for specialist support; to Pat Lawton for letting me rewrite her childhood; to my mother, for books that arrived by train, and insisting I learn to knit "properly"; to my aunts Rita and Bessie, both knitters, who bequeathed me my grandmother's Bakelite knitting needle box; to my daughter Elisabeth who continues the tradition; to the countless other friends with whom I have shared love and knitting, but particularly Chimene O'Rafferty, Cathie Sharp, Bev Priest, Maureen Harris and my sister Beryl; to Ian Bone, Lesley Williams, Ray Tyndale, Jan Harrow, Mandy Treagus, Julie Ireland, Patrick Allington, Malcolm Walker, Tony Bujega, Sabina Hopfer, Christopher Lappas, Carol Spencer, and Robin and Aileen Spiglioni-Beiers for sharing the writing journey; to Laurel Carpenter and Yvonne Elson and my mother again for their prayers. And thanks be to God.

The Jane Austen Book Club

Karen Joy Fowler

In California's Sacramento Valley, six people meet once a month to discuss Jane Austen's novels. They are ordinary people, neither happy nor unhappy, but all wounded in different ways, all mixed up about their lives and their relationships. Over the six months they meet marriages are tested, affairs begin, unsuitable arrangements become suitable and, under the guiding eye of Jane Austen, some of them even fall in love ...

'This exquisite novel is bigger and more ambitious than it appears. It's that rare book that reminds us what reading is all about.'
The New York Times Book Review

'A thoroughly delightful comedy of contemporary manners.'
Entertainment Weekly

AMANDA BROOKFIELD

THE SIMPLE RULES OF LOVE

For some families, a year can feel like a lifetime . . .

The Harrisons are a large and extremely close-knit family. But with the grandchildren fast becoming adults and elderly Pamela struggling to adapt to widowhood and the emptiness of Ashley House, the four children of the middle generation find themselves equally lost in a changing world.

As preparations for forty-two-old Cassie's long-awaited wedding gather pace and an exotic family holiday is planned, sibling and marital bonds are stretched to breaking point: adultery, an unwanted pregnancy, shadows of past losses . . . suddenly a year of celebration threatens to become one of painful upheaval.

Beset by such emotional chaos, how can the adults hope to guide their children in matters of the heart? Or are the children the ones who should be guiding them?

A multi-generational story of love, lies and family ties. *The Simple Rules of Love* presents Amanda Brookfield at her perceptive and poignant best.

Coronation Talkies

Susan Kurosawa

In Chalaili, an Indian hill station stranded above the clouds, where the trees and flowers are of ravishing hues and the annual monsoon hits with monumental force, a small enclave of British expatriates cling to the glory of a fast-fading empire.

Into this faltering world come two starkly different but memorable women: the larger-than-life Mrs Banerjee, with her armoury of gold bangles and saris in thrilling colours, and Lydia Rushmore, a timid Surrey school teacher hurriedly married off to the town's disgraced meteorologist. Mrs Banerjee sets out to transform the rundown Chalaili theatre into Coronation Talkies, a thoroughly modern cinema showing Hollywood's latest love stories. Lydia Rushmore discovers the soothing effects of gin as she tries to fit into hill station society and please her complicated new husband.

As World War II looms in Europe and British colonial power recedes, Chalaili becomes the setting for trickery, seduction and the unveiling of shocking secrets.

A charming comic debut novel of love, lust and lies

SHARON OWENS

THE TEA HOUSE ON MULBERRY STREET

Daniel Stanley might make the most glorious desserts in Ireland, but he won't support his wife **Penny's** desire to have at least one bun in the oven. And the owners of Muldoon's Tea Rooms aren't the only ones hoping for change.

Struggling artist **Brenda** sits penning letters to Nicolas Cage and dreaming of a better life; **Sadie** finds refuge from her husband's infidelity in Daniel's famous cherry cheesecake; and **Clare** returns home from twenty years in New York, still cherishing the memory of the one night she truly loved – and lost. And **Penny** herself discovers a secret from the past – and a sexy estate agent very much in the present.

They all want their lives to change – but are they willing to face the possibility that you can't always have your cake – and eat it?

'By entwining romance with food, Owens does for cakes and coffee what Joanne Harris did for chocolate' *Big Issue*

'A delightfully warm read you'll devour in one sitting' *Company*